ALABAMA BLAST FURNACES

THE LIBRARY
OF ALABAMA
CLASSICS

ALABAMA BLAST FURNACES

Joseph H. Woodward II
New Introduction by James R. Bennett

The University of Alabama Press
Tuscaloosa

Originally published by Woodward Iron Company, Woodward,
Alabama

Woodward II, Joseph H.
New introduction by James R. Bennett
Alabama blast furnaces

Library of Alabama classics.
ISBN-13 978-0-8173-5432-9 (pbk. : alk. paper)
ISBN-10 0-1873-5432-8 (pbk. : alk. paper)

Cataloging-in-publication data available from the Library of
Congress.

INTRODUCTION

Alabama Blast Furnaces, Joseph H. Woodward II
Woodward Iron Company, 1940

James R. Bennett

IN the thirty-year period following Ethel Armes's classic history of the Alabama iron and steel industry in 1910, very little was written of a substantive nature about more recent developments in the iron trade. That was until Joseph H. Woodward II, an executive with Woodward Iron Company in Birmingham, spent the better part of 1940 filling in missing parts of the epic story that set Alabama apart from all its sister states.

Armes and Woodward were both keenly aware that Alabama possessed vast mineral wealth, especially those resources needed to make iron. At no place else in the world could all of the ingredients for its manufacture—iron ore, limestone and coal—be found in such close proximity. The various ores and fossil fuels hidden by primordial upheavals within the valleys and ridges of Alabama's Appalachian Plateau invited investment in great centers of manufacturing. Due to lower manufacturing costs and reduced transportation needs that these mineral resources provided, new industrial cities like Birmingham, Bessemer, and Sheffield sprang to life.

Woodward, the grandson of J. H. Woodward, one of the founders of the Woodward Iron Company in 1881, lived in the most promising of these places—Birmingham—a city yet forty years old at his birth. He was the son of A. H. (Rick) Woodward, former Woodward Iron Company president and board chairman and owner of the Birmingham Barons. His mother, Annie Jemison, was the daughter of Robert Jemison Sr., the first president of Birmingham Railway, Light and Power Company and a former Confederate senator.

As a teenager, Joseph H. Woodward II (1912–65) attended Phillips Academy in

Andover, Massachusetts, and later Yale. He joined his father's company in 1934 working in the Purchasing Department. During World War II, he served as a captain in the U.S. Army Air Corps when, while stationed at Santa Ana, California, he married Lt. Mary Ellen Massebean, a member of the Army Nurse Corps, on May 11, 1944.

After the war, they returned to Birmingham, where he re-joined Woodward Iron as the company's forestry engineer. He would go on to serve as "attorney in fact" at the iron plant, as assistant to the president, and secretary of the company. After his father's death in 1950 he was named to its board of directors and as director of public relations in 1951.

Active in the Birmingham civic community, Woodward also served on the board of directors for the First National Bank, Allied Life Insurance Company, and the Jefferson County Community Chest. He remained with the iron company that bore his name throughout his business career.

Woodward, who tried his hand at fiction, also wrote several historical articles including *Alabama Iron Manufacturing, 1860–1865* published in the July 1954 issue of the *Alabama Review*. The paper was first read on April 30 of that year at the Seventh Annual Meeting of the Alabama Historical Association in Birmingham. Woodward served on the association's executive committee.

His most notable work was *Alabama Blast Furnaces*, a well-received review of the Alabama iron industry, published by the Woodward Iron Company in 1940. In that effort Woodward did prodigious research and wrote the text. He was assisted by H. A. Berg, then the company president and former president of Sloss-Sheffield Steel & Iron Company, and Henry J. Noble, a department manager at American Cast Iron & Pipe Company (ACIPCO). Many photographs used in the work unfortunately have been lost over time.

Written to provide a record of every blast furnace built in Alabama from 1815 to 1940, the Woodward book was widely acclaimed and today remains as one of the most quoted historical references on the iron and steel industry of the period.

On receipt of her copy of *Alabama Blast Furnaces* on November 23, 1940, Ethel Armes, then living in Washington, D.C., wrote Berg that she was "perfectly delighted" to have it and called the work "a valuable record." "At the time I started my research on coal and iron in 1907, data was available from very few resources—scarcely any of those noted in your book," she said. "Nothing at all then, from the Public Library in Birmingham. The information had to be gleaned from unpublished sources and by interviews with the old men long on the ground.... Your company's book takes me back over the years," she added. "It was all a great adventure."

Woodward specifically thanked Ms. Armes in his acknowledgements, saying he was indebted to her research "for much valuable data."

John H. Adams, a veteran of the Birmingham iron industry who opened and operated a number of early iron ore and coal mines in the area, acknowledged receipt of his copy of the book on November 15, 1940, calling it "the greatest addition to the metallurgical history of our state to this time." Adams, who was instrumental in having the Vulcan statue built for the 1904 St. Louis World's Fair, came to Birmingham in 1880 as superintendent of the Birmingham Rolling Mill Company.

"I congratulate you on the result of your work in gathering therein so much real data that has been lost or hidden from the people of Alabama for so long."

Woodward began working on the book early in 1940 and by February was seeking information from newspaper editors and historians in far-flung corners of the state. By August, he was pulling together the last of the photographs and illustrations.

Out of print for more than sixty-five years, copies of Woodward's book have become prized possessions in many public and private libraries. The reprinting of *Alabama Blast Furnaces* by the University of Alabama Press fortunately makes this detailed history of Alabama's most important nineteenth- and twentieth-century industry available once again to citizens everywhere. I think Mr. Woodward would have liked that. His work lives on.

An avid hunter and fisherman, he traveled extensively but loved to return to Birmingham and his home in Mountain Brook. He died unexpectedly at age 53 on June 25, 1965, at his summer house at Sapphire Lake, North Carolina, and is buried at Birmingham's Elmwood Cemetery.

At this writing one daughter still lives in Birmingham, Mary W. Oestenstad, and another, Anne W. McKee, resides in Cashiers, North Carolina. Described by his nephew, A. H. (Rick) Woodward III, as a "warm and wonderful man," the accolade seems a fitting tribute to the iron company executive who so masterfully chronicled Alabama's iron industry from the dark days of the Civil War to an era of national importance at the onset of World War II.

By 1940, the year he wrote *Alabama Blast Furnaces*, 40 percent of the foundry iron produced in the United States came from the Birmingham District—the same year Woodward Iron Company ranked as the largest independent manufacturer of pig iron in the country.

References

Armes, Ethel. *Story of Coal and Iron in Alabama*. 1910. Reprint, New York: Arno Press, 1973.

Birmingham Post, March 26, 1942, February 21, 1949, July 25, 1941.

Birmingham Post-Herald, June 26, 1965.

Historic American Engineering Record, Library of Congress.

Personal correspondence, A. H. Woodward III, Birmingham, June 28, 2006.

Surname Microfilm File, Alabama Dept. of Archives and History, Montgomery, Alabama.

Woodward II, Joseph H. *Alabama Blast Furnaces*. Alabama: Woodward Iron Company, 1940.

Woodward Family Papers, W. H. Hoole Special Collections Library, University of Alabama.

Woodwards WeSearch Newsletter. Vol. 2, no. 2 (January 2003).

ALABAMA BLAST FURNACES

FOREWORD

The manufacture of pig iron in Alabama is the most important industry of the State and is a vital factor in the prosperity and welfare of its people.

Many books, trade journal articles, newspaper articles and much statistical data regarding this subject have been published from time to time and are available in libraries, company files and in the public archives. But, for the busy participant in the industry itself or for the interested layman, a record of all blast furnaces built and operated in Alabama, is wanting.

It is to fill this want and to present a general picture of the development of iron making in Alabama that we have ventured to put forth this volume. Many documents, records and drawings have been studied; many individuals have been consulted and all other available sources of information have been carefully traced and considered in order to approach as closely as possible the authentic facts.

We take pleasure in presenting this book as our contribution to the records of our state and to the records of the great industry of which we are proud to be a part. We hope that it may serve to help keep alive the spirit of initiative and progress so characteristic of all American industrial pioneers.

H. A. Berg,
Woodward Iron Company.

ACKNOWLEDGMENTS

Acknowledgment is made to the following individuals and organizations for their contribution to the planning and production of this volume:

Mr. Joseph H. Woodward II of Woodward Iron Company, who gathered the data and wrote the text.

Mr. Henry J. Noble of Birmingham, Alabama, who inspired production of the chronicle and contributed valuable advice in its preparation.

The Birmingham Public Library, the University of Alabama, the State Department of Archives and History, the U. S. Department of the Interior and Department of Commerce, the Birmingham Chamber of Commerce and Birmingham newspapers from the files of which much of the historical material was obtained.

Acknowledgment is also made to the personnel of these various institutions and organizations as well as to the many individuals associated with the development of Alabama's iron industry, who have generously assisted by supplying information incorporated in this volume. For much valuable data we are also indebted to "The Story of Coal and Iron in Alabama" by Miss Ethel Armes.

CONTENTS

INTRODUCTION

History of iron making in the State of Alabama covers a period of one hundred and twenty-five years. This history may be divided roughly into four divisions:

The first, or "Pioneer Era," extending from the building of the first blast furnace in Alabama in 1815 to the outbreak of the Civil War in 1861.

The second, or "War Period," covering the four years of the Civil War from 1861 through 1865.

The third, or "Reconstruction Era," extending from 1866 to the advent of the modern furnace in 1879.

The fourth, or "Modern Period," embracing the years from 1880 to the present.

These divisions of time were not abrupt cleavages. Each period merged gradually with the one which followed, leaving an indelible imprint. Each poured its contribution into the mould of Alabama's iron industry and helped to cast its present-day stature.

PIONEER ERA

1815-1861

IN 1815—four years before Alabama was admitted to the Union—the first blast furnace was erected in the state.

So closely integrated with community life was this and other blast furnaces built during this pioneer era of Alabama's iron industry, that any chronicle of these iron makers must be set against the frontier background of this early period in the state's history.

In 1815, and for many years thereafter, North Alabama was a frontier where life was crude and extremely simple. Much of this section of the state was then a wilderness. Cherokee, Chickasaw and Creek Indians still roamed the forests. Such settlements as had come into existence were largely along navigable rivers. These were self-contained communities in most of which were found a blacksmith shop, a tanyard and a general store. Transportation was largely by river, despite floods and drought. Such roads as existed were impassable during much of the year to all but the man on horseback. Steamboats plied upstream to bring the products of civilization and returned downstream with raw materials from the frontier. As early as 1824 they carried cargoes up the Tennessee river to the shoals at Florence. An interesting sidelight on the price of importations from New Orleans is furnished by this price list of commodities, published in the "Enquirer" of Tuscumbia in 1824:

Flour	$8.00	bbl.
Salt	1.50	bu.
Whiskey	.40	gal.
Sugar	.15	lb.
Coffee	.40	lb.
Iron	.10	lb.
Steel	.31	lb.

Also interesting as an index of the population characteristics of the period is the census of Tuscumbia in 1827 which listed:

White males over 21	365
White males under 21	185
White females over 21	184
White females under 21	183
Blacks	403
	1320

From 1815 to 1861, life ran on in Alabama like a slow moving stream. Settlements expanded, population grew, scattered industries came into existence, virgin forests gave way to farms. But on the whole, this entire period brought little basic change to the pattern of life in Alabama or the status of the state's iron industry.

Like the life in Alabama, blast furnaces of this early era were very simple in design. All had certain similarities of construction.

Most of these early isolated operations had forges. Here the cold blast charcoal iron was beaten into plow points, fire dogs and other domestic implements. If the plant was far enough removed from other settlements, a sawmill and grist mill were usually built. One such early plant boasted a machine shop "capable of executing the finest workmanship." As a rule, however, the ingenious blacksmith was more than capable of making and maintaining the simple machinery of the furnace.

These early blast furnaces were owned either by individuals or partnerships, rarely by a stock company. Despite this individuality of ownership, Alabama never had a "mansion furnace," so common in Virginia, where the furnace was usually operated in conjuction with a plantation; in Alabama the furnace was the main object.

A furnace 30 feet high with a 6 foot diameter bosh was capable of producing from three to eight tons of pig iron a day, depending largely on the grade of ore. If the owner was not an iron-master, he hired an operator who was paid according to the tonnage of iron produced. These early iron manufacturers had no knowledge of chemistry, no analysis of the ore or charcoal; they depended on some ancient formula which they altered to suit local conditions. The iron-master stood on the top of his little stone stack amid the pulsating billows of smoke and sparks and gauged by eye the amounts of ore, fuel and limestone required.

At casting time he stood in the high arch covering the iron notch and directed the cast. From the forehearth the iron was tapped into small sand beds or, if hollowware was being cast, the iron was ladled directly into the molds. When a sufficient quantity of domestic and agricultural implements had been cast, they were hauled by wagon throughout the surrounding country and sold or bartered to the farmers and small store owners. Quite often these wares were rafted down some river to larger towns. Most of the pig iron was shipped to small foundries, forges, gin manufacturers and other small users of iron.

The usual shape of the furnace was that of a truncated pyramid built of stone blocks around a hollow chamber, the height ranging from 19 to 40 feet and the bosh (the widest portion of the chamber) from 4 to 8 feet in diameter. The location of the furnace depended upon four equally important factors: first, the proximity of an ore bed (usually surface ore); second, a stream sufficient to furnish water power for blowing; third, an abundance of wood for burning into charcoal; and fourth, a hillside against which to build the stack. This last requisite was essential for the charging of the raw material into the furnace top. For this purpose a bridge was built to connect the furnace top and the hill.

By comparison with the modern blast furnace plant, the old furnace seems a marvel of simplicity. It must be remembered, however, that virtually all of the material as well as the appurtenances of the plant had to be obtained locally. As a rule the large limestone blocks, forming the outer portion of the stack, had to be cut and hewn by hand, then hauled by oxen to the furnace site. It may be assumed that a large part of the manual labor was performed by slaves. That does not imply that the furnace owner (iron-master) was himself a slave holder. The practice was to hire slaves from local owners on a yearly basis. The operator, by contract, housed, fed, clothed, and guarded the slaves, a practice which continued until the end of the Civil War.

Due to the necessity of locating the furnace near the ore, the plants were often some distance from the nearest settlement. Under such circumstances, little self-contained communities arose in the furnace neighborhood. Log houses first were built to house the labor, then usually a small store was operated by the iron-master to supply the essential commodities.

Between 1815 and 1860 only two improvements of importance were made in blast furnace practice. In 1854 the first hot blast pipe stove was installed in Alabama. It is interesting to note that this innovation was declared a failure by the first man to use it. The second innovation was the substitution of steam driven blowers for the older water power. With water power, the operation of the plant depended on the supply of water, consequently during times of drought or flood, the furnace was idle.

Therefore, this latter improvement enabled the furnace to operate a much greater portion of the year.

Prior to the Civil War seven (and possibly eight) stone blast furnaces were built in Alabama. We are accustomed to the veneration of anything historical; in fact, we think of the pioneer as a hero. In a certain measure the pioneer ironmaster was a courageous man but in his own eyes (from the evidence of his records) he was simply a business man working under somewhat annoying handicaps. These little furnaces were nevertheless the stepping stones to our modern plants.

THE CIVIL WAR ERA

1861-1865

OVER the peaceful scene in Alabama, long-hovering war clouds broke in 1861. One by one the Southern States seceded, the Confederacy was formed, the tragic Civil War ensued. At the outset both the Union and Confederacy anticipated a brief war and a decisive victory. During the first year of hostilities, importations from abroad provided a large part of the Confederate army ordnance. But when the war entered its second year, the military needs of the South became increasingly apparent as the Union blockade grew more effective. Soon the South realized that immediate development of its manufacturing facilities was imperative. As the conflict wore on, "iron and more iron" became the pressing cry of the Confederacy.

On April 11, 1862, the Confederate Government established the Nitre and Mining Bureau to foster the production of raw materials for its various arsenals. At the commencement of the Civil War there were six, or possibly seven blast furnaces operating in Alabama. The total daily capacity of all these furnaces could not have exceeded 40 tons and was probably less. As the war dragged on, the armies in the field demanded more and more supplies of shot and shell. More and more iron became an absolute necessity and the Nitre and Mining Bureau put forth increasing effort to supply the deficiency. Finally the shortage of materials became so acute that the Confederate Congress, on June 16, 1863, passed an act empowering the Nitre and Mining Bureau to impress all manufacturing.

Nitre and Mining Bureau,

SELMA OFFICE.

In accordance with General Orders, No. 30 and 32, A. & I. G. Office, the following regulations will be observed by Contractors with this Bureau.

I. All detailed men and conscripts leaving their work or refusing to work, will at once be turned over to the nearest Enrolling Officer to be tried and punished as Deserters.

II. Any Contractor hiring the operatives of another Contractor, without his written consent, will be immediately reported to this office; and if the operative so employed, is not at once discharged or returned to his employer, all detailed men and conscripts will be at once removed from the works of the offending party, and such other action taken as will effectually prevent a practice so destructive to the interest of all.

III. No subsequent employment of the operative, so discharged, will be permitted without the consent of the original employer be first obtained.

IV. No transfer of detailed men or conscripts from one Contractor to another will be permitted, even with the consent of all parties, until such transfer is first approved by the Officer in charge.

The Major in command will use all the power with which he is clothed to prevent interference with the employees of one Contractor by another, either by the offer of higher wages or otherwise. It is a practice eminently calculated to destroy the whole Iron interest, and it is hoped Iron Masters will not resort to such devices.

WM. RICHARDSON HUNT,
Major &c. on Ord. Duty, in charge of Iron and Mining of Ala., Ga. & Tenn.

Confederate Nitre and Mining Bureau bulletin issued to Alabama Iron Masters in 1863.

Between 1862 and 1865 thirteen new blast furnaces were built in Alabama. The Confederate government advanced either all or part of the funds necessary for these projects. Amounts up to $100,000 were provided and, in return, the operators were required to furnish definite percentages of the furnace output to the arsenals and shipbuilding yards. Under the stress of war conditions, the Nitre and Mining Bureau dictated the operating policies of the blast furnace industry. Owners, operators, labor—both skilled and unskilled—were pressed into service.

Governmental regulations multiplied and became most stringent. Reports of every kind had to be filled in and filed; the detailed information required was almost endless. Added to these difficulties was the continued scarcity of operating essentials such as labor. The Confederate government pressed thousands of slaves into service to dig trenches and perform similar tasks in the combat areas. Union raids freed thousands more. The labor shortage became acute.

Horses, mules and oxen could be obtained only through government orders. Staple food supplies, such as meat, corn and hay had to be brought in from Florida and other distant points. Due to the lack of labor and supplies, furnaces often had to shut down for weeks at a time.

Financial difficulties also beset the furnace operator during this period. At the beginning of the war the price of iron ranged between $25 and $30 a ton. Slave hire was $125 to $175 per year. As the war progressed the credit of the Confederacy weakened, inflation of the currency took place and by 1865 iron was quoted at $500 per ton, a meaningless figure since the currency was practically valueless.

By that date slaves had almost disappeared and the lot of the ironmaster was far from a happy one. In the the end it mattered little; profiteers and patriots suffered the same fate.

In spite of these odds and difficulties, during the war years two notable experiments were made by Alabama furnacemen. Pig iron was produced in Shelby County using raw bituminous coal as fuel, the result being pronounced "the equal of hot blast charcoal iron." In Jefferson County the first coke pig iron in Alabama was produced, the experiment being proclaimed "a success." That neither experiment was carried further was due to the lack of a coal supply. A permanent advance made during the war years was the first installation in Alabama of a manually operated bell and hopper on the furnace top.

FURNACE AND MINE RETURN up to *Octo 1st 1864*

Contractor's Names	*do*	*Shelby Iron Co*
Name of Works	*do*	*Shelby Iron Works*
Location of Mines	*do*	*Five miles south of Columbiana Ala*
Number of Men Detailed	*57*	*Sixty five (65)*
Number of Men Exempt	*11*	*Eleven (11)*
Number of Negroes Employed	*261*	*Two hundred sixty one (261)*
Total number of Hands employed	*329*	*Three hundred & thirty seven (337)*
Tons of Iron at Furnace last Month	*743* 383	*Three hundred eighty three*
Tons of Iron Produced this Month	*418* 377	*Three hundred seventy seven*
TOTAL	*10.94* 760	*Seven hundred sixty*
Tons of Iron delivered	*743* 58	*Fifty eight*
Tons of Iron at Furnace this date	702	*Seven hundred two*
Tons of Coal at Mines last Month	41	57
Tons of Coal raised this Month	743	261
TOTAL		329

Form of Nitre and Mining Bureau report which was required of all Iron Masters under contract
with the Confederacy.

Confederate States Naval Station,

Selma, Ala., January 5th 1863.

SIR:

There is required in the *Construction* .... Department *on Tombigbee River*

on account of *Iron Clad Rams* for

Two (2) Tons of (½) half inch square Iron

Two (2) Tons of 3/4 inch Round.

Two (2) Tons of 7/8 inch Round.

one (1) Ton of 5/8 inch Round.

one half (½) Ton of 1¼ inch and a quarter Round

Respectfully submitted, ... Respectfully, *Porter & Watson*

Approved, *Julius A Pratt m*

Senior Officer

Received the above mentioned articles for

.... Department.

To

OOB 38

Paymaster,
C. S. Naval Station, Selma.

Confederate requisition for iron to be used in construction of iron clad rams on the Tombigbee.

Following is a list of the furnaces known to have supplied pig iron to the Confederacy:

	Furnaces
Cane Creek	1
Shelby Iron Co.	2
Round Mountain	1
Choccolocco Iron Works (Knight)	1
Roup's Valley Iron Works (Tannehill)	3
Hale & Murdock Iron Works	1
Red Mountain Iron & Coal Co. (Oxmoor)	1
Cahawba Iron Works (Irondale)	1
Bibb Naval Furnaces	2
Salt Creek Iron Works (Jenifer)	1
Oxford Iron Co.	1
Cornwall Iron Works	1
Little Cahaba Iron Works	1
	17

Dut to the many irregularities of operation at this time it is impossible to estimate the tonnage produced. A report of the Nitre and Mining Bureau to the Confederate Congress states that twelve furnaces operating in Alabama delivered to the government in the nine month period ended Sept. 30, 1864, a total of 5913.7 gross tons of pig and rolled iron. And the total iron delivered to the government from Jan. 1, 1863 to Sept. 30, 1864 amounted to only 12,354.8 gross tons. Another report, dated Nov. 20, 1864, to the Chief of the Nitre and Mining Bureau states:

> "In one case the government furnace in Bibb County, Alabama, averaged through the month thirteen tons of iron per day, and at another furnace an average of ten tons per day was obtained for one month. From many disturbing causes incident to the war much time has been lost at the Alabama furnaces and the daily average would scarcely exceed, if equal, four tons per day."

Despite the smallness of this amount, Alabama delivered to the Confederacy more iron than the rest of the Southern States combined.

Gen. Robert E. Lee surrendered on April 9, 1865 and the war was practically over. In the deep South, however, Union raids still continued. At Munford, April 25, 1865, the last shot was fired in defense of Alabama. The Home Guard was overcome and a momument now marks the spot of the last Alabama casualty. Two miles farther the raiders came upon the little furnace on Salt Creek and destroyed it. Only one of Alabama's 17 furnaces was left intact. Dark indeed seemed the future of the iron industry in Alabama.

THE RECONSTRUCTION ERA

1866-1879

THE years which followed in the wake of the Civil War have been called the "tragic era" in the South's history. That four-year conflict left Alabama and other Southern states stripped of wealth and resources, with almost every industry paralyzed and prostrate. To this bitter cup of defeat was added military rule and martial law with "carpet bag" and "scalawag" control of state governments to impede further restoration and recovery.

For eight years after the war's end, the iron industry of Alabama lay practically dormant. But then within a single year, four new companies were formed and four furnaces were built, largely with Northern capital. During this Reconstruction Era, there was also introduced a new type of furnace construction, employing iron or steel shells with iron supporting columns instead of the old type of stone furnace, only two of which were built after the war. In this new type furnace, sandstone hearths and open tops continued to be used at first, but these were soon changed to fire brick hearth and lining and closed tops, of the bell and hopper type. Steam driven elevators took the place of the old hillside method of filling. Steam blowing engines replaced the old water driven blowers. Oxen could no longer be employed to transport the larger quantities of base material and increased volume of products. Railroads were built and new markets were opened. At last the industrial star of Alabama seemed to be in the ascendency, when suddenly the panic of 1873 descended on the nation. Southern enterprises suffered a severe setback. Hopes fell and the fight against vast odds seemed once more hopeless. Not all men despaired, however, and from the panic of 1873 came an experiment that finally turned the tide of fortune for the iron industry of Alabama.

The cost of charcoal iron, even in 1873, was too high to compete with cheaper Northern coke iron. Only for specialized castings was charcoal iron used. And too, with each succeeding year charcoal became scarcer and more expensive as forests surrounding furnaces were gradually depleted.

In the Fall of 1875 it was decided to use Alabama coke to smelt Alabama red hematite ore. Perhaps the iron-masters had forgotten the experiment during the Civil War. At any rate there was divided opinion on the practicability of this new move. In February, 1876, however the first cast of coke iron was made. Opinion still remained divided; some declared the iron a success, others ridiculed the attempt. Northern iron-masters proclaimed the coke iron a "wretched product;" the Southern press replied with glowing forecasts for the future of Alabama's iron industry. Finally after four years experience with production of coke iron in the Birmingham district, further capital was attracted and confidence was established. Two modern furnaces were started. The Reconstruction Era was over and the Alabama "Iron Boom" was under way.

THE MODERN ERA

1880 - 1940

IN 1880 the first two coke furnaces in Alabama went into blast. Building of these plants and their successful operation may be considered the beginning of modern pig iron manufacture in Alabama, which up to that time had been merely a minor charcoal iron producing state. Opening near Birmingham of two immense coal fields in close proximity to vast ore bodies made these furnaces possible assuring an abundant and dependable coal supply.

Following the opening of these coke furnaces in Birmingham enthusiasm ran high. The Southern press was jubilant and filled with optimistic predictions. Northern interests sent representatives to Birmingham to confirm the miracle—a mountain of ore on one side and an almost inexhaustible supply of coal on the other. All agreed that the mineral development of the state was assured a bright future. Alabama was pictured as a place where nature had bestowed her favors with a lavish hand.

This favorable publicity produced its effect. During the next five years the state's iron industry progressed at a reasonable rate. In these years, five more furnaces were built in the Birmingham District. These also prospered and soon tales of bonanza spread far and wide. Optimism rose to high levels, and presently the great Alabama "Iron Boom" was in progress.

Between 1886 and 1890 twenty-seven blast furnaces were built in Alabama. Glowing reports induced the flow of capital from all sections of the country. New towns came into being; old towns assumed boom proportions. Land speculation, corporate promotions and stock selling became the order of the day. Railroads furthered the fantastic scheme. Not only did they contribute to furnace projects, they often fostered them by guaranteeing cheap rates to Northern markets. Every blast furnace was pictured as a gold mine and the world was invited to participate in the expected flow of profits.

The years from 1886 to 1895 witnessed the construction of more blast furnaces in Alabama than any other period in the state's history. The whole nation became Alabama conscious. This is not a period, however, to which Alabama can look back with pride. Many of the furnaces constructed during this boom time were failures, marked today only by piles of slag. All too often furnaces were projected to enhance local property values. Too many were built upon a foundation of optimistic speculation rather than factual knowledge.

In 1907-08 there were no less than fifty-one completed blast furnaces standing in Alabama. From that date the number has steadily decreased. In 1939 two furnaces were dismantled to leave but 19 remaining in the entire state.

Over-expansion during the boom period was most unhealthy for the state. Alabama, as an iron producing district, fell into disrepute. Gradually, however, the weaker concerns were weeded out. Numbers of consolidations took place in which the stronger companies absorbed the less strong. Some of these consolidations were also ill-conceived and eventually failed. Furnaces which had been built without regard to such factors as markets, raw material supplies or transportation were abandoned. Gradually order supplanted chaos and stable conditions finally prevailed.

During the sixty years from 1880-1940 great advances were made in all phases of the Alabama iron industry. In the field of labor a marked change took place. In 1880 there were 1500 men employed in the industry who worked an average of 76 hours a week. In that year (1880) a total of 68,995 gross tons of pig iron were produced. Today there are approximately 15,000 men employed in the manufacture of pig iron in Alabama who produce nearly 3,000,000 gross tons yearly. There was in 1880 a chronic local shortage of skilled labor. As a consequence for a number of years skilled men were imported from Northern and Eastern plants to run and maintain the Alabama blast furnaces.

Here it is interesting to note that the industry pays today approximately $1.00 per ton in corporate taxes, whereas in the year 1887 it paid only $0.026 per ton of iron—a sum only 1/40 as much.

Market conditions also greatly changed during these 60 years. In 1880 more than 90% of Alabama iron was shipped to Northern localities.

Slowly this situation altered. By 1910 the South was absorbing 20% of the production. Pressure and soil pipe industries, stove manufacturers and other consumers of iron were established in the South with the result that today local Southern markets take from 60 to 70% of the South's merchant iron, the remainder being shipped by rail or water to the foundry markets of the nation or abroad.

The change from charcoal to coke fuel permitted the construction of larger furnaces. The Northern and Eastern iron trade promised a ready market for the increased tonnage and so, during this era of expansion, larger furnaces were built. Coal and ore properties were further developed or acquired and closer attention was given to securing raw material reserves for the future.

Enormous technical advances were also made during this era. Alabama furnaces kept step with development in other sections of the country.

Enlarged furnaces stepped up production of iron per unit from around 100 tons per day to 800 tons on the larger stacks. To handle the charges for these larger furnaces, skip or mechanical filling entirely replaced the old hand filling method. Mechanical devices for distributing the stock in the furnace were adopted to produce a more regular and uniform operation. Modernized stock houses were built to facilitate the rapid handling and accurate charging of the furnace burden.

Hot blast stoves of various modern design took the place of the old type pipe stove, thus producing higher heats and better fuel economy. Blowing engines of the old and crude design gave way to the newer and more efficient types of engines and turbine driven blowers. Surplus gas from the furnace and formerly wasted coke breeze from the coke ovens were utilized to produce power in modern generating stations for outside use or in the nearby ore and coal mines.

Slag or waste cinder from the furnaces was prepared for useful commercial purposes. Pig iron from the furnace was no longer cast into sand beds but handled through hot metal ladles over modern pig casting machines, eliminating back-breaking labor and producing a greatly improved and uniform product.

A most important development during this period was the continually increasing use of chemistry and research to promote the accurate control of the output and the discovery of new products and new uses for old products. Control equipment of various types and kinds for all phases of furnace operation was put into general use, enabling the manufacturer to produce grades of iron according to exacting and definite specifications.

By-product coke ovens displaced the old beehive ovens with the resulting benefits of a better and more uniform quality coke and the recovery of formerly wasted products such as gas, tar, sulphate of ammonia and motor benzol, to mention only a few. Closer attention was given to the proper preparation of raw material before charging into the furnace. Ores were crushed, screened and sized; coke crushed and screened to produce a clean and uniform fuel with resulting marked improvement in Southern blast furnace practice.

All these many developments not only made the task of labor far easier, they contributed to shorter hours and greater earning power. The standard of living for Southern iron producing labor was elevated to the level of that in other parts of the nation.

Not only has the Alabama iron industry in recent years progressed apace with the rest of the country, it also has taken the initiative in applying modern air conditioning apparatus to the control of moisture in the air blast. Elimination of moisture in the blast was attempted early in the present century and its benefits realized, but equipment of that time proved uneconomical. With apparatus now available, this further refinement in furnace control has proved successful.

These painstaking efforts in preparing raw materials for the furnace—ore, coke and even the air itself; the intelligent use of the most efficient equipment and control apparatus and an alert and progressive personnel, enable the Alabama merchant producer of this modern day to provide an ample and dependable supply of highest quality pig iron.

And so ends the present story of the "modern era" of iron production in Alabama. Fruitful of accomplishment as have been these past sixty years, this modern era should be viewed as the beginning of a period of still greater progress which will reach far into the future. Like the century and a quarter which encompasses the life history of Alabama's iron industry, it seems certain that the future of the industry will also be witness to many changes and perhaps still greater changes than the past has seen. It seems certain, too, that in this future there will also come alternating periods of progress and recession. But of the ultimate destiny of Alabama's iron industry there can be no question. That destiny was decreed aeons ago, when Nature stored huge reserves of coal, ore and limestone in close proximity in Alabama and cast here the mold of a great industry.

SUMMARY

SEVENTY-SEVEN blast furnaces have been built and operated in the State of Alabama. Four more furnaces were either partially completed or, if completed, were never operated. Out of this total of 81 furnaces 32 were built to use charcoal as fuel and of this number 10 used coke at some time during their operation. Five of these 11 furnaces were later permanently converted for coke fuel. Since 1877 forty-eight furnaces have been built to use coke.

Today there are 19 blast furnaces in the state. Seventeen of these are located in the Birmingham District. Eighteen furnaces are active at this writing; the nineteenth has been idle for a number of years due to its state of repair and an uncertain raw material supply situation.

The question may well be asked as to why this decrease in the number of units. There are several answers. The first furnaces were very small with very limited productive capacity. They depended on local ore and fuel sources for their supply of raw materials and on local narrow markets for the disposal of their products. As time went on demands for iron increased, new furnaces were built, each of greater size and capacity. As in the case of many other industries, the principle of mass production asserted itself. With larger units and larger production, costs could be lowered. However, with larger furnaces, greater capital was required, wider markets had to be sought and a dependable supply of ore and fuel in much larger quantities became necessary. Consequently location and transportation became increasingly important factors. The transition from "small business" to "big business" took place. Larger and stronger organizations were necessary, hence the various consolidations or mergers during the past fifty years. Increasingly severe competition also fostered the gradual concentration of productive facilities into the more economically sound, ably managed and adequately financed concerns, controlling ample and favorably located raw material supplies and reserves. Such organizations were also better able to finance and adopt the most up-to-date improvements and developments in the industry and so to keep pace with the other iron producing sections of the country.

Numbers of the older furnaces were forced out of existence because they had been built without due regard to the various involved economic factors. Others failed through lack of financial resources. Still others failed because they were originally conceptions of speculative enthusiasm. It will be noted in the records that a number of furnaces operated intermittently, with long periods of idleness between operations. These may be termed fair weather furnaces. Their building was induced by a nearby supply of ore but their fuel had to be obtained from distant localities and consequently their competitive position was greatly weakened. Such plants were able to operate only in times of abnormal demands and high prices. They had no stable position in the industry. After the period of great demand for iron during the World War had passed, these furnaces were gradually abandoned and scrapped.

And so it is, that while at one time there were thirty or more merchant pig iron companies in Alabama, today only three survive. The decrease in the number of furnace units does not indicate a decrease in productive capacity. On the contrary, the total annual output of the remaining furnaces is greater than the many smaller plants formerly operated.

The surviving merchant blast furnaces of Alabama have consolidated their position. As a result of intelligent operation, they compete successfully in the nation's markets. With the combination of ample material reserves, efficient modern plants and sound financial structures, their position is assured. The foundry industry of the country can be certain of a dependable Alabama pig iron supply, manufactured under close specification limits to suit individual or special needs. The development of inland waterways and the combination of rail and water rates have helped to bring Alabama pig iron economically closer to a widespread area of the nation.

Approximately 40% of the foundry iron consumed in the entire country is now furnished from the Birmingham district; Alabama's proportion in 1912 was approximately 20%. This is factual evidence of this state's increasing importance in the national picture as a pig iron producing center.

INDIVIDUAL HISTORIES OF ALABAMA BLAST FURNACES

ON the pages which follow the individual history of every blast furnace built in Alabama from the year 1815 to 1940 is presented. Included are those furnaces which were constructed but never put in blast and those on which construction was abandoned before their completion. The record is arranged in alphabetical sequence for the more convenient reference of the reader.

Alabama City Furnace.

ALABAMA CITY FURNACE
Etowah County (near Gadsden)
January 17, 1904

IN 1898 the Alabama Steel & Wire Company was formed and a small wire mill erected in Ensley, Alabama. This company obtained its supply of steel from the adjacent works of the Tennessee Coal, Iron and Railroad Company and prospered for several years, to such extent that it decided to expand and make its own steel. Accordingly, a tract of land was purchased two miles west of Gadsden, Ala., and late in 1902 the building of a blast furnace and steel plant was started. This new furnace was 90 feet high and 20 feet diameter in the bosh and was considered a rather large stack at that time. The furnace was blown in on January 17, 1904. Coke was first shipped from the Birmingham District but sometime later 200 beehive ovens were built at the plant and 300 more ovens were constructed at the company's Virginia Coal Mine in Jefferson County. In 1918 the Sayre Coal Mine was purchased to supplement the Virginia mine.

Ore was obtained first from the red hematite vein in Etowah County near Attalla, and from brown ore deposits in the same locality and in Cherokee County. In 1914 land was purchased on Red Mountain near Birmingham, and in 1921 the Shannon Mine was opened.

For several years billets were produced and shipped to the wire mill in Ensley. In 1909-10 the wire mill was removed to Alabama City.

In 1906, due to depression conditions, the Alabama Steel & Wire Co. was forced to reorganize. The Southern Steel Co. was formed which took over the Alabama Steel & Wire Co. and also the Trussville Furnace Co. property. The panic of 1907 caused the failure of the Southern Steel Company and it was reorganized into the Southern Iron and Steel Co. In 1911 the Alabama Consolidated Coal and Iron Co. proposed a merger with the Southern Iron & Steel Company but the English security holders of the latter company objected and it was placed under the receivership of Jas. Bowron. At that time the Trussville Furnace property reverted to a Northern bank through foreclosure.

In 1913 a corporation, the Standard Steel Company, was formed to purchase the defunct Southern Iron and Steel Company at public auction. In December 1913 the newly formed Gulf States Steel Company assumed ownership. This latter company operated until 1937 when it was merged into and became a part of the Republic Steel Corporation and is now known as the Gulfsteel Division of that corporation.

The Alabama City furnace was blown out June 26, 1928 and a new stack was built and blown in on Sept. 17, 1928. This new stack, erected in less than three months, was 92′ high, 16′ hearth diameter and 21′-7″ bosh diameter with an annual capacity of 175,000 gross tons. The furnace was idle for several years prior to 1937 but has been in blast since that time. Coke is supplied from 37 Koppers ovens of 16-18 tons capacity each, which were built in 1916. Output of this furnace is charged into the open hearth furnaces for steel making.

"Big" and "Little" Alice Furnaces in Birmingham in 1885.

ALICE FURNACES
Birmingham, Jefferson County
No. 1 Nov. 23, 1880
No. 2 July 24, 1883

IN 1879 Col. H. F. DeBardeleben and T. T. Hillman formed the Alice Furnace Co. with capital of $80,000 and on Sept. 29, 1879 ground was broken for erection of the first furnace (Alice No. 1) within the limits of Birmingham, and the fourth to be built in Jefferson County. The plant was located on First Avenue north just west of 14th Street. The furnace was blown in Nov. 23, 1880. Dimensions of the stack were 63′ x 15′ and the average daily output for the first year was 53 tons of foundry iron—a record for that time.

The Alice Furnace Co. in 1881 absorbed the Hillman Coal and Iron Co. and the Birmingham Coal and Iron Co.* and increased the capital to $250,000. A second blast furnace (Alice No. 2) 75' x 18', was erected and put into blast July 24, 1883. This furnace, in 1886, established a 24 hour production record for the South of 150 tons.

In 1884 Enoch Ensley of Tennessee consolidated the Alice Furnace Co., Linn Iron Works and Pratt Coal and Coke Co. into the Pratt Coal and Iron Co. Two years later, in 1886, the Tennessee Coal, Iron & Railroad Co. acquired the Pratt Coal and Iron Co. and with it the two Alice furnaces. Again, in 1907, the property changed hands when the U. S. Steel Corporation acquired the Tennessee Coal, Iron & Railroad Company.

One hundred and fifty beehive coke ovens were built at the furnace in 1879-80 to coke Pratt coal and later an additional one hundred ovens were added.

Red hematite ore from Grace's Gap on Red Mountain, furnished by the Morris Mining Co., was first used; later the ore was mined on the company property at Redding and Hillman.

No. 1 Alice, or "Little Alice," was dismantled in 1905 and the No. 2 Alice was abandoned in 1927 and dismantled in 1929.

The No. 1 Alice Furnace made the first basic pig iron in the Birmingham District which was suitable for open hearth use. A pamphlet published in 1897 makes the following statement: "The Alice Furnace ran on basic iron over a continuous period of more than twelve months and during that time supplied almost every steel works of any importance in the country," and, "it is a fact that not even a single ton of the iron was rejected by the customers." The success of this run was a contributing factor in the decision to build a steel plant at Ensley.

The original Alice Furnace was extremely important in the development of the Birmingham district because its success convinced Northern capital that the manufacture of iron with coke in Birmingham was practical. Both of the Oxmoor furnaces had been converted to coke from charcoal but their performance was not impressive. The Edwards Furnace in Bibb County had been blown in a few months prior to the Alice but was using brown hematite ore. It remained for the Alice furnaces to prove to the iron industry that Alabama coke and red hematite ore produced a good grade of foundry pig iron.

---

*Not to be confused with later company of same name. See Vanderbilt furnace.

ATTALLA FURNACE

(Known also as The Eagle Furnace)
Attalla, Etowah County
June 10, 1889

THE town of Attalla, once the site of an important Indian village, is situated about five miles due west of Gadsden in the county of Etowah. Here in 1888 the Southern Iron Co. of Nashville, Tenn. began the construction of a small charcoal blast furnace for the purpose of utilizing the local red and brown hematite of both Etowah and Cherokee Counties. This furnace went into blast June 10, 1889. Its stack was 55' high and 11' across the bosh. Charcoal was made at the furnace but this supply was supplemented by outside contracts. The company owned very little ore property and depended largely on local mining contractors.

Due to this situation and the low price of pig iron the furnace was blown out in the summer of 1892 and remained idle until 1900.

In 1895 the Buffalo Iron Co. of Nashville, Tenn. acquired the property but did not attempt to operate the furnace. The Eagle Iron Co. of Chattanooga, Tenn. bought the plant in 1900 and after repairing the furnace put it into blast in the Fall of that same year. New charcoal kilns, with an annual capacity of 2,400,000 bu. were built.

The Attalla furnace remained in blast from 1900 through most of 1907, making pig iron for the car wheel trade. The plant had an annual capacity of 18,000 tons, most of which was consumed by the various car wheel companies of Alabama and Tennessee.

After the furnace had been idle for almost a year the property was sold in 1908 to T. S. Kyle, but within six months the plant was taken over by the First National Bank of Chattanooga. On Dec. 30, 1909 the Eagle Furnace Co. bought the property and after some minor improvements on the stack put the furnace into blast in the late Spring of 1910. The operation was not economically practical and after a run of little more than a year the furnace was blown out and remained idle from 1910 until the World War. The Gulf States Steel Co. leased the plant in Dec. 1916 and operated the furnace with coke until the lease expired in April, 1919. The stack was dismantled in 1924-25.

Battelle Furnace. This view was made just before completion of furnace in 1904. Lookout Mountain in background.

BATTELLE FURNACE
DeKalb County—near Georgia Line
Sept. 10, 1904

THE Lookout Mountain Iron Co. was organized in April 1902 with a capital stock of $1,000,000 with the intent of developing a tract of 15,000 acres of ore and coal land. Most of this capital was raised in Ohio and some of the best known men in the iron business invested in the company and served on its board or directors. The Lookout Mountain Iron Co. was the last company organized in Alabama to erect a merchant blast furnace.

The site chosen for the blast furnace was in Wills Valley in eastern DeKalb County not far from the Georgia line. At this point the valley is about one-quarter mile wide, with Lookout Mountain on one side and Ore Ridge on the other. The coal (Eureka or Rattlesnake seam) outcrops on the side of Lookout Mountain and the ore (fossiliferous red hematite) outcrops on the Ore Ridge. Adjacent to the furnace was built a battery of beehive ovens. The raw material haulage distance at this plant was the shortest in Alabama, being not more than a half mile. On paper the Battelle Furnace (named for the president of the company) was the most economical plant in the South and perhaps in the world. However, within eighteen months after being blown in, the furnace was shut down and never again operated. Abandonment was due in part to the "squeezing out" of the coal from 36″ on the outcrop to less than 24″ at 1000 feet, and in part to the discovery that the ore was excessively high in alumina.

The Battelle Furnace was begun in the Spring of 1903 and put into blast Sept. 10, 1904. The stack was 85 feet high and 19 feet in the bosh. "The bosh jacket is provided with four auxiliary tuyeres to be used in the removal of scaffolds, should these occur."

In 1905 the Battelle property was acquired by Cincinnati interests. The furnace was blown out in 1906 and remained idle until 1917 when the plant was dismantled, sold and shipped to the Tata Iron Works of India.

Approximately $1,000,000 was expended at Battelle and a total of 80,000 to 85,000 tons of pig iron were produced.

BAY STATE FURNACE
Fort Payne, DeKalb County
Abandoned 1891

THE town of Fort Payne in DeKalb County became for a few years the Mecca of New England capital. Within the short space of three years no less than $5,000,000 was spent here in the building of industries.

At the height of this activity the Bay State Furnace Co. was organized on April 19, 1890 with capital of $250,000. About 3/5 mile east of the Bay State Furnace, the Fort Payne Furnace was nearing completion. Both stacks were the same, 65' x 14'. At the Bay State Furnace was a battery of beehive ovens to coke the coal mined on the company land a few miles north. The ore, both red and brown hematite, was located on a ridge ¼ mile west of the furnace and brought to the stock house in trams.

In 1891 the Fort Payne Furnace failed because the coal did not coke well and the ores were very inferior. Since the Bay State furnace planned to use the same raw materials, it was clear that this venture was also impractical and work on the Bay State stack was accordingly suspended.

The partially completed Bay State furnace was bought by the Bessemer Land & Improvement Co. in 1895. The Directory of the American Iron & Steel Institute of 1896 states: "furnace may be completed at Fort Payne by the present owner or it may be torn down and removed to Bessemer." This project was abandoned and the plant was dismantled in 1898-99 by a Canadian firm for scrap.

The Bay State was one of the furnaces which was never completed and with the nearby Fort Payne furnace was one of the unfortunate ventures undertaken without sufficient consideration and induced by the wild speculative fervor of the time.

Practically everything that was built at Fort Payne during those years (1888-1891) has disappeared: the rolling mill, the brick plant, the Ft. Payne & Eastern RR. and many smaller enterprises.

As has been noted, the vast majority of the money came from New England. In this connection, it is related that some time after the Fort Payne failure, two Civil War Veterans were reminiscing about the War and the Yankee said, "We sure gave you Rebels hell at Gettysburg."

"Yes," the Confederate agreed, "but we sure got even at Fort Payne."

BESSEMER FURNACES
Bessemer, Jefferson County

Bessemer Furnaces
No. 1—1888
No. 2—1889

Robertstown Furnaces
No. 3—1890
No. 4—1890

Little Bell Furnace
No. 5—1890

FIVE blast furnaces have been built in the City of Bessemer, Jefferson County, Ala. Three companies began the work but their history is identical after the first year or so. Under these circumstances it will be clearer to treat the five Bessemer furnaces as a unit rather than as separate enterprises.

Two furnaces were on the west side of Bessemer and became known as the Robertstown Furnaces; about a quarter mile south of these was the Little Bell Furnace, and about one mile southeast of the Little Bell were located the two Bessemer Furnaces. First two of these furnaces were built by H. F. DeBardeleben and associates who formed the De-Bardeleben Coal and Iron Co. in 1886 with an authorized capital of $2,000,000. Bessemer Furnace No. 1 was blown in during June 1888 and in April of the following year the No. 2 furnace was put into blast. Both stacks were 75' x 17' and made approximately 100 tons a day each.

In 1888 the Bessemer Iron & Steel Co. was formed for the purpose of erecting two more furnaces. On July 23, 1888 a third company, The Little Bell Iron Company was incorporated and the fifth furnace was begun.

On Dec. 10, 1889 the three aforementioned companies (The De-Bardeleben Coal & Iron Co., the Bessemer Iron & Steel Co., and The Little Bell Iron Co.) were consolidated into the DeBardeleben Coal & Iron Co. The capital stock of the consolidation was authorized at $10,000,000. Stockholders of the original DeBardeleben Co. received approximately 71% of the new stock; those of the Bessemer Iron & Steel Co. a little more than 23% and the stockholders of the Little Bell Iron Co. only about 5½%. It was stipulated that no profits were to be distributed among the stockholders of either the Bessemer Co. or the Little Bell Co. until their plants were completed and in operation.

Robertstown Furnaces. This picture was taken about 1895.

Bessemer Furnace No. 2 as it appeared about 1890.

Little Bell Furnace during progress of construction in 1889.

The following year, 1890, the two Robertstown and the Little Bell furnaces were put in operation. The Robertstown Furnaces (later known as the Bessemer Furnaces No. 3 and No. 4) were the same size as Bessemer furnaces Nos. 1 and 2, viz., 75′x17′. The Little Bell (usually called the Little Belle through error) became the Bessemer No. 5. This furnace was the smallest of the five stacks, being 60′ high and 12′ in the bosh, and was originally designed to use either coke or charcoal; the latter fuel, however, was never used. Most of the ore used by the Bessemer furnaces was red hematite from a mine below Jonesboro on Red Mountain; some, however was from Trussville, north of Birmingham. All this raw material was hauled to Bessemer via the L & N RR.

Concurrently with the construction of Bessemer Furnaces (No. 1 and No. 2) 275 beehive ovens were also built. These coked coal from the DeBardeleben Company's Blue Creek mine.

On June 1, 1892 the Tennessee Coal, Iron & Railroad Company acquired all the holdings of the DeBardeleben Coal & Iron Company, exchanging its securities for those of the DeBardeleben Company at the rate of 8 to 10. In 1907 the Tennessee Coal, Iron & Railroad Company became a part of the United States Steel Corporation and the Bessemer furnaces changed hands again for the last time.

After the Bessemer furnaces were acquired by the Tennessee Company, the red ore was supplied from that company's own mines just east of the plant on Red Mountain. Coal was furnished from the Tennessee Company's Blue Creek mines and coked at the furnaces. By this time 300 beehive ovens had been built at Robertstown and the total number of ovens at Bessemer No. 1 and No. 2 furnaces had been increased from 275 to 420.

In 1906, the Little Bell (Bessemer No. 5) was blown out and lay idle almost ten years when it was pressed into service during the World War. The Little Bell operated throughout the war period but was permanently blown out in February 1919, finally being dismantled in 1927. The remaining four furnaces in Bessemer were operated fairly regularly until completion of the two furnaces in Fairfield during 1928. In the following year Bessemer No. 1 and No. 2 were dismantled and No. 3 and No. 4 (Robertstown Furnaces) were dismantled in 1935.

BIBB FURNACES

(Known also as Brierfield, Strother,
and Bibb Naval Furnaces)
Bibb County, near Brierfield
No. 1—1861
No. 2—1863

THE State of Alabama seceded from the Union on Jan. 11, 1861 and during the turbulence and confusion of this same year, Bibb County's second blast furnace was constructed under the leadership of C. C. Huckabee and Johnathan Newton Smith, who organized the Bibb County Iron Co. for that purpose. This furnace was two miles from the town of Ashby and little more than a mile from Short Creek. J. N. Smith contributed his knowledge and experience in the iron business and Huckabee furnished the capital and his negro slaves. This little stone stack was 36' high and 10½' in the bosh.

At first the iron was used for general agricultural and domestic purposes but as the war wore on, the need for iron became more acute. The blast furnace companies of the state—of the entire South—were put under contract to supply the Confederate government. A contract was offered by the Confederacy to the Bibb County Iron Company but was refused. With the arsenal at Selma consuming almost all the iron produced, the planters were in desperate need and were willing to pay far above the government price. The Bibb Company was unwilling to sacrifice such lucrative trade on the altar of patriotism and continued to decline the Confederate contract. As a consequence of this refusal, the Confederacy purchased the property at a "force sale" the price being $600,000 in C. S. A. money. Maj. W. R. Hunt, Chief of the Nitre and Mining Bureau at Selma, assumed command. The Confederacy in 1863 began the construction of a large brick furnace (Bibb Furnace No. 2) 40' high and 11-1/3' in the bosh equipped for hot blast. The new plant became known as the Bibb Naval Furnace with A. E. Mott in charge.

Ore used at the Bibb furnace was exclusively brown hematite and was mined within a few miles of the plant. The charcoal came from the pine forests of the neighborhood.

The entire output of this furnace went to Selma and a good portion was used in plates for the Confederacy's iron clad gunboats. Most of the iron, however, was cast into large naval ordnance for which it became famous.

Bibb Furnace in Bibb County, built in 1863, blown out in 1894. An earlier stone stack built in 1861 stood adjacent to this furnace.

Because this plant was owned by the Government, it did not experience the great shortage of both skilled and unskilled labor which was so often the case in the other furnace plants since both classes of labor were detailed from the Army.

The Bibb Naval Furnaces continued to produce iron for the Government until April 1865 when they were partially destroyed by Gen. Wilson, who was marching through Bibb County on his way to Selma.

The Federal Government confiscated the property as contraband of war and in 1866 put it up for public sale. Francis Strother Lyon and associates purchased the plant and immediately put Gen. Josiah Gorgas, former Chief of Ordnance for the C. S. A., in charge. Repairs were made and operations were resumed late in 1866.

On Jan. 28, 1867 the Brierfield Iron Works Co. was incorporated. This included not only the furnaces but also the destroyed rolling mill which was located about three miles east of the Bibb furnaces. . The operation did not prove to be very successful, due in part to the inexperience of the managers and in part to the lack of market. Hence the furnace was leased to T. S. Alvis and Company on Aug. 2, 1869 on a $3.00 a ton royalty basis. The Alvis Company operated the plant until the panic of 1873 when the furnace was blown out. It remained idle from 1873 until it was purchased on Feb. 1, 1877 by the Messrs. Carter of Louisville, Ky., who partially rebuilt the stack and put it into blast.

In 1881 the Brierfield Coal and Iron Co. was formed to purchase the Bibb property and Maj. T. J. Peter was elected president. The company rebuilt the furnace to 55' x 12' and spent considerable money on the rolling mill and on a new nail factory. Shortly after, the cut nail began to be supplanted by the wire nail and once more the plant became idle. In 1886 the furnace was remodeled to use coke. This was not, however, the first time that coke was used in the Bibb Furnace as evidenced by the following statement of the Geological Survey of 1875:

> "Coal from the Lemley vein used in the puddling furnace at Brierfield, and coke made from the same coal mixed with Charcoal was used, with poor results, in the blast furnace."

Beehive ovens were built at this time at Brierfield to coke coal from the company mine located on the "overturned measures."

After about a year operations ceased and through foreclosure proceedings the Alabama Iron and Steel Company acquired the property in 1888 and in 1890 converted the furnace back to the use of charcoal.

The Southern Mineral Land Company took over the property in 1894 through another foreclosure. The furnace was blown out in that year and was never again operated. The property is owned today by the Southern Mineral Land Corporation, successor to the Southern Mineral Land Company which was declared a bankrupt in 1932.

There is some controversy as to the probability of two blast furnaces having once been at Bibb. None of the older inhabitants can recollect the original stone stack. Evidence of its existence is contained, however, in this record written in 1866 by an engineer who visited the plant:

> "Alongside this furnace (the hot blast) stands the old cold blast furnace, which has not been in blast since the close of the War."

The existence of two stacks is also mentioned as late as the 1880 Directory of the Iron and Steel Association.

IRON WORKS.

THE subscribers have bought J. M. Moore's interest in the CANE CREEK IRON WORKS, and have made, and are still making, large improvements on the Furnace and Machinery.

We are now prepared to make Hollow ware, DOG IRONS, GIN GEAR, and *MIL MACHINERY* generally.

Such as Cranks,
Wing Gudgeons,
Concave Gudgeons,
Rods, Ways, Rack,
and Pinions;
Noddleheads, and Saw Mill Irons of ALL SORTS for WATER MILLS.

Also, heavy Gearing for Mills, and Light Gear for Smutters, Bolts, and Elevators, Spindles, Balance Irons and Drivers, Couplings, and Pullies, and can have them all turned and fitted up ready for use.

Also Morris' celebrated

Cast Iron Water Wheels,
for Factories, Saw Mills, Grist Mills, Cotton Gins, &c., also, Hotchkiff's and Centervent, water wheels.

IRON Columns, Bases, & Caps, Window Sills, and Lintels, Balustrade, Window Wrights, Cellar Grates, &c.

Particular attention paid to the getting up Patterns.

Country Produce, such as Pork, Bacon, Wheat, Corn, &c., taken in payment.

☞ Forty or Fifty industrious laboring men can have EMPLOYMENT here at all times.

Address, GOODE, MORRIS & Co.
MORRISVILLE, Benton Co., Ala.
Aug. 22, 1855.—tf

Reproduction of advertisement published in Jacksonville Republican in 1855 offering a wide variety of castings made at Cane Creek Furnace in Calhoun County and seeking workmen.

CANE CREEK FURNACE

(Known also as Hades Iron Works, Benton County Iron Works,
Goode & Moore's Iron Works, Old Polkville Furnace,
Crowe's Iron Works)

Calhoun County, near Anniston
1840

JACOB STROUP, descendent of Pennsylvania iron-masters who had cast cannon for the Continental Army during the American Revolution, built the second blast furnace in the State of Alabama. Jacob Stroup is credited also with having built the first iron works of both South Carolina and Georgia. Some time prior to the election of William Henry Harrison in November 1840, as President of the United States, Stroup blew in his little stone furnace, using charcoal as fuel from nearby forests and ore from adjacent deposits.

The following advertisement appeared in The Alabama Reporter, Talladega, Alabama, and is the first record of the early enterprise:

> *"Alabama Reporter"*
> *Nov. 7, 1844*
> *Iron, Castings, Etc.*
>
> The subscribers are now prepared at their Iron Works on Cane Creek in Benton County, to furnish their friends and the public in general with all sorts of castings, and iron of every description.
>
> HOLLOW WARE, COGS, MILL IRONS, TIRE IRON, and castings, for machinery of every sort, will constantly be kept on hand or supplied at the shortest notice.
>
> Persons wanting any of the above irons will please apply at the Iron Works or to Mr. H. M. Cunningham in Talladega, where samples can be seen.
>
> *Noah Goode & Co.*
> *Hades Iron Works, Benton County*
> *Sept. 26, 1840*

Stroup built the plant and operated it for a short time, then sold it to Noah Goode who had come from Georgia to Alabama with the iron-master as assistant and bookkeeper. Goode lacked the capital to operate the plant and sold an interest to Dr. John M. Moore of Talladega, who supplied not only the necessary capital but some 50 slaves. There is in existence an account of one of these slaves being killed by a rock fall in the ore pits, the first recorded fatality in the history of Alabama's iron industry.

The following is a letter written by one of the proprietors to J. D. B. DeBow, which recites in detail the conditions during that period:

"Polkville, Benton Co., Ala.
Sept. 26, 1849

We have a blast furnace, a puddling furnace, and forge, in operation. We turn out daily about 6000 pounds of iron, 2000 pounds of which we put into hollow-ware and machinery castings, 2000 pounds into bar iron, and 2000 pounds into pigs. We use 600 bu. of charcoal every 24 hours. Our iron ore beds (some of them) are within 600 yards of the furnace. Our limestone is at the furnace and in abundance. The nearest Stone Coal Beds that have been worked, are thirteen miles off. We are now preparing to put up a rolling mill, and think that in a short time we will be able to roll iron successfully. Our establishment is five miles East of the Coosa River, opposite the Ten Islands, and eleven miles from Greensport. We ship our iron down the Coosa in flat boats to Wetumpka, Montgomery and Mobile. We have found the articles we produce here of a ready sale in either of those markets. We are prepared to make, turn off, and fit up, all kinds of machinery, except fine castings for cotton mills and will be very soon ready to furnish them."

On Feb. 10, 1852, Noah Goode and John M. Moore incorporated by act of the legislature the Benton County Iron Works, with $100,000 capital. On Nov. 19, 1855, E. G. Morris bought Moore's interest in the Cane Creek property and the firm name was changed to Goode, Morris and Company. During the Civil War the old plant changed hands and became known as Crowe's Iron Works.

The original furnace was 32 feet high and 7 feet across the bosh. At the time the furnace was built a rather novel, but not original method of blowing, was used. A wooden box some 12 feet square by 20 feet high was placed under a fall on the creek. The top of the box was closed except for an opening in the center 1 foot square. Into this was placed a wooden square pipe through which water poured, sucking in air at the same time. This air, under a little pressure, was piped to the furnace through a 3 inch opening in the side of the box. This method was changed in a few years to the more conventional water wheel and tub blower.

Before the Civil War hollow-ware and other articles cast at the furnace were hauled throughout the surrounding countryside and sold or bartered to farmers and storekeepers.

A considerable amount of iron was shipped via river to the Janney Foundry at Montgomery in 1847. At that time Janney was furnishing the iron for the building of the State Capitol. During that same year iron was shipped from Cane Creek to Mobile and cast into ordnance for use by the Federal government in the war with Mexico. J. P. Lesley in 1858 gives the following particulars about this plant:

> "Height 32', Bosh 7', built 1843, rebuilt 1857. In 1854 produced 450 tons in 41 weeks run, in 1855, 350 tons in 35 weeks, and in 1856, 350 tons in 30 weeks. Hot blast removed in 1856-7; to be replaced in Fall of 1857. Ore, 2/3 brown hematite and 1/3 honeycomb, from Chalybeate Springs bank 2 miles North of furnace, and from six other openings in the same neighborhood. Makes No. I and II grey foundry iron for Montgomery, Mobile, and New Orleans markets, and castings for home market."

In the same bulletin there are listed two forges in connection with the "Polkville" furnace:

> "No. 1 makes blooms for No. 2; has one shingling hammer. No. 2 has a Catalan hammer and makes bars from puddle blooms from No. 1. These two forges run only in winter as there is not enough water in summer for all the works."

The Confederate States of America, shortly after the outbreak of hostilities, contracted for the output of the Cane Creek Furnace. The iron was shipped by river steamer either to the arsenal at Rome, Ga. or to Selma. At the latter arsenal, the iron was rolled into armor plate and used on the farmous Confederate gun boat, Merrimac.

After a continuous operation of almost 25 years, the historic Cane Creek furnace was destroyed by a party of Federal Cavalry raiders under Gen. Lovell H. Rousseau on July 14, 1864.

CEDAR CREEK FURNACE

(Known also as Alabama Iron Works, Old Napier)
Franklin County, near Russellville
1815

IN 1815 the armies of Napoleon were defeated on the field of Waterloo and a semblance of peace was restored to a war weary Europe. On January 8, 1815, the makeshift army of Kentucky and Tennessee volunteers under Gen. Andrew Jackson defeated the British at New Orleans in the last battle of the War of 1812.

Some time during that memorable year, the first blast furnace was built in what is now Alabama. A young Pennsylvania iron-master, Joseph Heslip, left his native state in 1812 and journeyed South into Tennessee. There for a time he engaged in the iron business with a kinsman by marriage, Anthony Wayne Van Lier, then again moved South. The exact date on which Heslip blew in his furnace is unknown, but one of Heslip's children was born at the Cedar Creek Iron Works in 1815 and is thus recorded in the family Bible. It was not until 1818 that Joseph Heslip bought clear title to his lands from the government at $2.00 an acre.

The little stone furnace was built about 5 miles west of what is now Russellville in the Chickasaw Cession of the Mississippi Territory, now Franklin County, Ala. The plant, of necessity, had to be as nearly self-supporting as possible and consisted of a forge, saw-mill and grist-mill.

The furnace was of the conventional style, a frustum of a pyramid, the base approximately 30' x 30', the top 25' x 25' and height 25'. Superimposed was a brick draft stack about 25' high making an overall height of about 50'. The stack was built of hand hewn stone and lined with hand made brick of local clay. From the evidence of other early iron-makers it is safe to assume that a major portion of the work was performed by slaves.

Brown limonite ore of the Lafayette formation was found on the surface site and hauled to the plant by wagon. The surrounding wilderness supplied an abundance of cheap wood which was converted to charcoal in pits and used as the furnace fuel.

In 1820 a plague, cholera it is supposed, swept the little community and caused the temporary abandonment of the property. Some authorities claim that the furnace was idle until 1822 when it was bought by Aaron Wells of Tennessee. It is more likely, however, that Wells purchased the plant on December 5, 1824, pursuant to a court sale as advertised in The Tuscumbian of Oct. 8, 1824, as follows:

"The Tuscumbian"
Oct. 8, 1824
Iron Works For Sale

"On Monday, the 5th day of December next, at the Alabama Iron Works, in Franklin County, State of Alabama, we will in pursuance of an order from the county court of said county, proceed to sell to the highest bidder, on a credit of one, two and three years, sixteen and one-half quarter sections of LAND, lying in Russell's Valley, on which is a furnace of the largest size and best construction, a FORGE, SAW-MILL and GRIST MILL. On said land is an inexhaustible quantity of IRON ORE, rich and of good quality, very convenient to the furnace. The purchaser or purchasers will be required to give bond and approved security."

It is probable that the furnace was held by Heslip until his death, at the age of 41 in 1824. For two years the plant was operated by Wells, then purchased by Dr. Robert Napier of Tennessee.

When the Cedar Creek furnace was permanently abandoned is a subject of controversy. There is proof that it operated during the year 1828 and one source says that it was in blast in 1837 but ceased during that year. Even the cause of abandonment is uncertain; some contending that the high cost of production and lack of transportation was the reason, and others that collapse of the stack was the cause.

At first the iron was cast in hollow-ware, fire dogs, and other domestic implements, as well as "pig-bars" for the smithy trade. The product was hauled throughout the surrounding countryside and sold or bartered to the farmers and smithies. Later when steam boats began to ply the Tennessee River a portion of the iron was shipped to New Orleans and transhipped to Liverpool, England where it commanded a price of $200.00 a ton. Depending on the stage of water on the river, the product was handled over land by oxen cart either to Chickasaw, 26 miles, or Riverton, 35 miles.

As testimony of the product and the craftmanship of those old ironmasters, there is preserved in Russellville, Ala., a large sugar kettle weighing 300 pounds, which after more than one hundred years of service, is in a perfect state of preservation. Once this large kettle fell from a moving truck to the concrete road and rolled down a steep embankment on to some rocks and suffered not a scratch.

COLE FURNACES
Sheffield, Colbert County
No. 1—Sept. 1888
No. 2—Oct. 1889
No. 3—April 1895

A PORTION of the land on which the three Cole furnaces were erected was granted by the United States in 1824 to Andrew Jackson and his brother James. In 1883 all the land now embraced by the city of Sheffield was acquired by the Sheffield Land, Iron & Coal Co., and in May of 1884 lots were put on sale and Sheffield was founded.

In 1886 the Alabama and Tennessee Coal and Iron Co. was organized with a capital of $2,200,000 and a few months later on Feb. 28, 1887 its name was changed to the Sheffield & Birmingham Coal, Iron & Railway Co. A tract of 60 acres, located in Sheffield and adjacent to the Tennessee River was deeded to the latter company for the purpose of erecting blast furnaces. The first furnace was blown in September 1888 and a second stack went into blast a year later in October 1889. Both furnaces were 75′ x 18′ and rated at about 170 tons a day each. Due to the shortage of coke in Alabama, these furnaces used Stonega Coke from Virginia. Brown hematite was acquired locally from Franklin County.

The affairs of the company became involved in litigation and in July 1890 the property was sold by a special master in U. S. Circuit Court. On November 4, 1891 a similar deed was made and the purchase price was stated as $350,000. The property was then deeded to the Alabama Iron and Railway Co. On Sept. 4, 1894 the property was deeded by that company to E. W. Cole and associates who, after June 27, 1895, operated the property under the name of the Sheffield Coal, Iron & Steel Co. This company completed the third stack which had been begun at the same time as the first two. This third furnace, the same size as the others, was blown in during April 1895.

In 1899 the three Cole Furnaces were leased by the Tennessee Coal, Iron and Railroad Co., which operated them from 1899 to 1903, using Pratt and Jasper coke from the Tennessee Company mines.

The Sheffield Coal and Iron Co. bought the property from the Sheffield Coal, Iron and Steel Company in 1903 and rebuilt all three furnaces. Once more the coke was obtained from Virginia and the brown hematite from Tennessee and the Russellville district.

Due to the high cost of fuel transportation, the plant operated but irregularly. In 1908 only two furnaces were in blast; in 1910 only one furnace operated and in the Fall of that year the last furnace was blown out.

The Cole Furnaces remained idle from 1910 until the World War. On Aug. 20, 1917 the plant was acquired by the Sheffield Iron Corporation. James Gayley, a former partner of Andrew Carnegie, was the head of the new company. The plant was mortgaged at this time to the Bankers Trust Co. of New York to secure a loan of $1,100,000. There was so much litigation connected with the transaction that operations were not commenced until some time in early 1918. The Porter Coal Mine in Jefferson County was leased and the coal was coked at the company's beehive ovens at Jasper. So much of the equipment had been disposed of that there was only blowing power enough to run one furnace. This furnace operated for the remainder of the war and was blown out in 1919.

When national prohibition went into effect the Valentine Brewery of New Jersey dismantled their plant and Gayley bought the refrigerating equipment for the purpose of installing a dry-blast system at the furnace. The idea was abandoned, however, and the machinery left on the furnace yard. Another idea of the same nature was partially developed. One of the unused stoves was fitted with a series of baffle-plates over which water, at a constant temperature of 68°, was to flow. The intent was to blow the air through this stove and reduce the moisture content prior to being heated. Before this could be tried the World War ended and operations ceased.

Shortly after the war the Bankers Trust Co. foreclosed its mortgage on the property. On June 11, 1923 the entire property was sold to the Sloss-Sheffield Steel & Iron Co. Two of the furnaces had been abandoned and dismantled between 1917 and 1920. The remaining stack became the Sloss Furnace No. 6. Sloss operated the plant intermittently until Aug. 19, 1927. Due to the high cost of fuel transportation (from Birmingham) the plant was abandoned and was dismantled between April 1934 and May 1935.

CORNWALL FURNACE
Cherokee County, near Centre
1862 or 1863

A S the Civil War entered the second year the Confederacy began to feel the lack of supplies. The Union blockade was strengthened from day to day and the importation of foreign munitions became more and more difficult. The armies of the Confederacy were proving their worth in the field but the supplies behind the lines were proving inadequate.

The Confederate States government was acquiring large field ordnance from the foundry and machine shop of the Noble Brothers of Rome, Ga. There was not, however, a sufficient supply of pig iron to meet the pressing demands of the ordnance department in Richmond. As a consequence, in 1862 the Noble Brothers, with the financial aid of the Confederacy, began the erection of a blast furnace in Cherokee County. The site chosen was about five miles west of Cedar Bluff on the Chattooga River.

Skilled artisans were detailed from the army and hundreds of negro slaves were hired from their owners. An immense amount of labor was required to complete the furnace. It was necessary to build a canal about half a mile long, then tunnel under the hill behind the furnace in order to supply the water power. The Chattooga River makes a long bend at this point and by means of the canal and tunnel, a drop of many feet was gained. The water power thus developed ran the blowing engines as well as a grist mill and flour mill.

All the machinery necessary to equip the furnace was built by the Nobles in Rome, Ga. and boated down the Coosa River to Cedar Bluff, then hauled overland to the furnace.

This plant, named "Cornwall" by the Nobles for their native county in England, went into blast either late in 1862 or early in the Spring of 1863. The ore used here (red hematite) was from Dirtseller Mountain, 3 miles away and was hauled to the stock house bank in two wheel carts. The ore was broken up into small pieces by slaves using sledge hammers. The charcoal was burned in the surrounding forests.

The entire output of this plant was contracted for by the Nitre and Mining Bureau of the Confederate States and most of it went to the foundry of the Nobles in Rome. Complete batteries were constructed here—cannon, carriage, and caisson. The Cornwall furnace produced from 5 to 8 tons a day and small as that appears, it was considered a fair average for that time.

Cornwall Furnace in Cherokee County. Note high main arch and bank in rear of stack.

Cornwall's usefulness to the Confederacy was limited. The Spring of 1864 saw the Union forces penetrating deep into the Confederate States. General Sherman called for reinforcements and Gen. Blair with the 17th Corps came from the West to join the Union army besieging Atlanta. On his march through Cherokee County, some time late in the Summer of 1864, Blair discovered the Cornwall furnace and destroyed all of it that would burn.

The history of Cornwall after the war is more or less a comedy of errors. The Nobles had met Col. Rattray in Rome in 1864 and were impressed with his ability. When it was decided to reconstruct the shops at Rome, they also determined to rebuild the Cornwall furnace. In 1866 the Nobles requested Col. Rattray to assist them in raising capital. The result was a partnership consisting of three men from Illionis and four of the Noble brothers. The plant was rebuilt and went into blast in 1867 as a cold blast charcoal furnace. Friction soon developed between the Northern and Southern partners, as a result of which, one of the Northern partners sold, in 1868, his $15,000 interest to Hugh McCulloch, a partner of the Nobles. Another of the partners sold his interest to Col. Wade S. Cothran, president of the Bank of Rome.

The entire capital stock of the company at that time was $60,000 divided as follows: Hugh McCulloch, $15,000; Kiser (of Illinois) $15,000; Cothran, $10,000; the Noble Brothers, $20,000.

Due to all the friction, the plant had been blown out in 1868 and the furnace was in need of repairs. Col. Rattray was placed in charge. The furnace was blown in during the first week in April 1869. Again friction arose and after three months Rattray resigned and Maj. Thompson took charge. "The expenses of the plant were increased $30 a day and never made to exceed 5 tons, and that was like silver, and pig thrown on the ground would break in two." At the end of six months, when the Major was dismissed, the plant was $30,000 in debt.

Early in 1870 William Noble took charge and shortly afterward the plant burned. There were thousands of bushels of charcoal stocked at the furnace and the intense heat caused "the stack originally built with lime rock to collapse into lime."

The Cornwall company then borrowed money from the Tredegar Iron Co. of Richmond, Va. to rebuild, and requested that a man be sent down to run the plant. A Mr. Patton, nephew of Tredegar's president, was sent and under his supervision a new stone stack, 44' x 9', was erected at a cost of $16,000. Patton operated the plant until late in 1872 when he was replaced by two furnacemen from Pennsylvania, "and by the time the company got a sufficiency of those two experts the works were sold for its debts."

The furnace lay idle for about a year, then J. M. Elliott supplied the money and in 1874 the plant was reconstructed under the supervision of "a Northern expert by the name of McElwane." Once again the plant proved economically unsound and sometime during the year 1875 the Cornwall furnace was blown out forever. It is today the best preserved of all the stone stacks now standing in the state.

DECATUR FURNACE
Decatur, Morgan County
Feb. 23, 1890

A NOTHER of the old towns of Alabama which experienced the great building boom of the 1880's was Decatur. This boom was begun in Decatur by the Decatur Land and Improvement Co., which company bought several thousand acres surrounding the town, then induced various enterprises to build, giving the factory sites. Among this number was the Decatur Charcoal and Chemical Co. which erected 48 kilns in 1887. In order to utilize the charcoal, the Decatur Land Improvement and Furnace Co. was organized and incorporated Feb. 21, 1887. From the Iron Age of Dec. 1, 1887 is reproduced the following account:

> "The furnace is to be 60 feet high and 12 feet across bosh, with two brick stoves. The work on the foundation of the furnace is going on, the cast house is building and stakes for the stockhouse have just been driven. Charcoal is to be delivered by the Decatur Charcoal and Chemical Co. at 5c a bushel in the stockhouse under a 10 years' contract. The ores are to come in barges from points on the Upper Tenn. River and from Murphy's Valley, where the company owns large tracts of ore and coal lands and into which the L. & N. R.R. is building a branch."

The furnace was completed in the Spring of 1888 and immediately was offered for sale or lease. At length, however, the furnace was blown in on Feb. 23, 1890, almost two years after being completed. For several months during 1891 the furnace used coke which was shipped from the Birmingham District.

Near the furnace was the plant of the Decatur Car Wheel & Mfg. Co., which had a capacity of 10,000 to 12,000 tons of pig iron a year. The L. & N. R.R. had also built shops and a foundry there. Despite all these apparent advantages, the furnace operated but a few years. When the panic of 1893 came, the railroads drastically curtailed their expenditures and the Car Wheel Works ceased operation.

The furnace was blown out in 1893 and was lighted only once again, in 1895, when it made a short run of less than one year. In 1898 the plant was bought by the Alabama and Georgia Iron Co. of which Eugene Zimmerman was president. Plans were made to operate the furnace but were abandoned. The Decatur Land Co. repossessed the property and dismantled the furnace plant in 1900.

EDWARDS FURNACE
Woodstock, Bibb County
June 10, 1880

G ILES EDWARDS, a Welshman whose family had been in the iron trade for many years in Wales, was a prominent figure in the iron industry of the South for amost 40 years. As early as 1860 Giles Edwards was superintendent of the first furnace in the Deep South to use coke in the making of pig iron. During the Civil War, he was Assistant General Superintendent at the famous Shelby Iron Co. in Shelby County, Alabama.

In 1873 Giles Edwards began the erection of a small charcoal blast furnace in the town of Woodstock, Bibb County. Near the furnace site were large deposits of brown hematite. Because Edwards attempted the task almost single handed, the work was painfully slow. At length, in 1879, the Edwards Iron Company was formed and sufficient capital was acquired to complete the furnace. The original furnace was designed to use charcoal; the new company enlarged the furnace to 55' x 12' to use coke. The capacity of the furnace was rated at 11,000 tons of "high grade mill pig iron."

The furnace went into blast June 10, 1880 and thus became the first blast furance in Alabama to be blown in on coke. The No. 1 Alice followed a few months later. A portion of the credit must go to H. F. DeBardeleben who helped finance the Edwards Iron Company and furnished coke (from the Pratt Mines) for several years on a cost, plus 10%, basis.

At the Edwards Furnace a rather unique method of raising raw materials to the furnace top was employed. The furnace was located in a valley and on the hill behind the stack was an abundant supply of water at an elevation greater than the furnace top. To each of the elevators, Edwards attached a wooden tub. When the elevator reached the furnace top, the tub was filled with water, which, with the empty stock buggy, over-balanced the loaded elevator on the ground and brought it to the top. At the bottom the water was emptied and the process repeated. The blowing engine at this plant was the old one which had been used at the Irondale Furnace, the fly wheel of which weighed 36 tons.

The furnace operated regularly until 1887 when it was blown out and remodeled. The stack was enlarged to 65' x 13½' and the capacity increased from 11,000 tons to 24,000. The furnace resumed operations but was blown out again in 1890.

H. F. DeBardeleben had supplied all the coke for the furnace and desired to have a larger interest in the operation. A decision was accordingly reached to enlarge the furnace again. Plans were made to build a railroad and open a coal mine and a portion of the road bed was graded. The furnace was remodeled and enlarged to 70' x 15' with a capacity of 30,000. Additional stock had been issued to raise the capital for these plant improvements. However when the furnace was ready to be blown in, some friction arose among the stockholders and the newly remodeled plant remained idle.

In 1895-6 H. F. DeBardeleben became president of the Edwards Iron Co. and in conjunction with the Bessemer Land and Improvement Co. planned to move the Edwards Furnace to Bessemer. The plan fell through and the plant was never operated after 1890. The property was finally purchased by the Martin Mining Co. and was later bought from this company by the Central Iron & Coal Co. The stack was dismantled in 1903-04.

The Edwards Furnace was actually the first stack in Alabama to be blown in on coke. Three other furnaces used coke prior to 1880 but each was an old charcoal furnace.

Battery of first four Ensley furnaces as they appeared in 1890. Note log cabins of employees in the foreground.

ENSLEY AND FAIRFIELD FURNACES
Ensley and Fairfield, Jefferson County

Ensley Furnaces

No. 1—April 29, 1889
No. 2—December 1888
No. 3—June 1888
No. 4—April 11, 1888
No. 5—November 15, 1900
No. 6—April 26, 1905

Fairfield Furnaces

No. 5—June 25, 1928
No. 6—September 27, 1928

IN 1885 the Pratt Coal and Coke Company was the largest holder of coal lands in Alabama and furnished almost all the coke then being consumed in the Birmingham District. In 1886 an option which had been secured on the Pratt holdings by a group of Tennessee capitalists headed by Enoch Ensley of Nashville, was exercised. The Alice Furnace Company and the Linn Iron Works were also acquired by these Tennesseans and a new company was formed, called the Pratt Coal and Iron Co.

Within a year (in 1886) the Tennessee Coal, Iron and Railroad Company, which was then operating coal and ore mines and blast furnaces in Tennessee, acquired the Pratt Coal and Iron Co. and increased its capital stock to $10,000,000. Acquisition of the Pratt Coal and Iron Co. marked the entrance of the Tennessee Coal, Iron and Railroad Co. into Alabama and this combination thereby became the largest and most important factor in the Southern iron and steel industry.

During 1886 (under the Pratt Coal and Iron Co.) a battery of four blast furnaces had been begun in the newly founded town of Ensley, a few miles southwest of Birmingham and within a short distance of the Pratt Coal Mines. Their construction was completed by the Tennessee Coal, Iron and Railroad Company. The four stacks were identical, 80' high and 20' in the bosh, with a daily capacity of 200 tons each. The first of these furnaces, the No. 4, went into blast April 9, 1888. The second stack, the No. 3, was blown in on June 5, followed by the No. 2 on Dec. 1, 1888 and the No. 1 on March 9, 1889.

The Tennessee Coal, Iron and Railroad Co. was now operating six furnaces (two Alice and four Ensley furnaces). On June 1, 1892 seven more stacks were acquired with the purchase of the DeBardeleben Coal and Iron Co., the five furnaces at Bessemer and the two Oxmoor Furnaces, making a total of thirteen stacks, the annual capacity of which in 1895 was rated at 633,400 gross tons. In order to supply this number of furnaces, new coal mines were opened on the Pratt Seam and additional beehive ovens were built at the mines. Through consolidation and purchase a large tract of ore land had also been acquired on Red Mountain.

In the Fall of 1897 the first battery of by-product coke ovens was begun in Ensley by the Semet-Solvay Company. This battery of 90 five-ton ovens was the first in the South and one of the first such operations in the nation. The ovens were built and operated by the Solvay Company. In 1899 thirty more ovens were built by this same company and in 1902 an additional battery of one hundred and twenty 6½ ton ovens was constructed.

In 1895 it was proved that basic iron could be produced in the Birmingham District and new markets were found among the independent steel manufacturers of the North and East. Shortly after basic iron was made commercially at the Alice Furnace, the Ensley steel mill was begun and went into production in November 1899. Success of this mill necessitated the erection of two additional blast furnaces to supply the iron for steel making.

The old Sewanee Furnace in Cowan, Tennessee, was dismantled in 1899 and removed to Ensley where it was set up as the Ensley No. 5.

This stack, smaller than the other Ensley furnaces, went into blast some-time in 1900. A sixth furnace was built at Ensley and blown in on April 28, 1905. A year later the small No. 5 was rebuilt to the same size as the new No. 6, 86'-7" x 20'-9", and blown in April 17, 1906.

The Tennessee Coal, Iron and Railroad Company had not been a financially sound company for some years prior to the time the panic of 1907 hit the iron industry of the nation. On one occasion it even had to mortgage its railroad in order to continue operating. The company's position in 1907 became critical and soon it was rumored that failure was impending. It was under these circumstances that E. H. Gary, President of the United States Steel Corporation, called on President Theodore Roosevelt to request permission to buy the practically moribund Ten-nessee Coal, Iron and Railroad Company. Gary contended that the nation could not survive another great business failure and Mr. Roosevelt agreed. In 1907 the entire property of the Tenneessee Coal, Iron and Railroad Company was acquired by the U. S. Steel Corporation for the sum of $35,300,000.

Since 1907, the company's six furnaces at Ensley have all been re-built and remodeled several times. As the capacities of the Ensley Fur-naces were increased, the outlying furnaces of the company (Oxmoor and Alice) were abandoned. In order to concentrate the entire property an additional battery of six blast furnaces was projected for the Fairfield operation (just west of Ensley) but to date only two of the six, No. 5 and No. 6, have been built. These two stacks, blown in during 1928, are each 95'-6" high, 23'-0" hearth and 27'-9" in the bosh. The Fairfield No. 5 and No. 6 are not only the most recent in the state but are also the largest. With the completion of these stacks, the last "outlying" furnaces (Bessemer Furnaces) were abandoned. In all the Tennessee Coal, Iron and Railroad Company has dismantled nine stacks in Alabama.

In 1912 the Tennessee Coal, Iron and Railroad Company built 280 by-product coke ovens and 363 additional ovens in 1919, 1920 and 1928. The last battery of 146 was built in 1937. The 120 Semet-Solvay coke ovens built in 1902 at Ensley are still in use and are believed to be the oldest active ovens in the United States.

Present annual capacity of the six Ensley furnaces and the two Fair-field furnaces is 1,612,750 gross tons. The greater portion of this iron is charged directly in a molten state to the open hearth furnaces for the mak-ing of steel.

The present Tennessee Coal, Iron and Railroad Company is the largest steel manufacturing unit operating in the South.

Etowah Furnace No. 1 as it appeared about 1890.

ETOWAH FURNACES
(Known also as Gadsden-Alabama Furnace)
Gadsden, Etowah County
No. 1—Oct. 14, 1888
No. 2—Aug. 22, 1903

THE Gadsden-Alabama Furnace Co. was formed in 1887 and work was commenced immediately on a blast furnace located on the east side of the town of Gadsden. On Oct. 14, 1888 this furnace was blown in. The stack was 75' high and 16' in the bosh; the annual capacity being rated at 35,000 tons.

This company owned 730 acres of "red ore and other lands," located near Attalla on the red hematite vein there. However, it had no coal, and purchased its coke requirements on the open market from Birmingham, Tracy City, Tenn., or Pocahontas, Virginia.

In 1893 the furnace was blown out due to the severe depression of that year. In 1896 the owners, T. T. Hillman, Geo. L. Morris and Mrs. Aileen Ligon, offered the property for sale or lease. In the formation of the Alabama Consolidated Coal and Iron Co. in 1899 this plant was included. About 1300 acres of additional ore land was purchased at that time to supply the Gadsden operation and the Ironaton Furnaces in Talladega County.

The furnace had been idle since 1893 and after general repairs had been made the plant went into blast late in 1900. The company owned coal mines and 375 beehive coke ovens in Tuscaloosa County (acquired from Standard Coal Company in 1900). In 1901 the coal mines of the Jefferson Coal and Railway Company in the Lewisburg district were acquired in addition to 250 coke ovens.

In 1902 a second and larger blast furnace was begun. This stack, 86′ x 19′, was blown in August 22, 1903. The No. 1 furnace was idle, its stoves and blowing equipment being used on the new No. 2. In 1905 the old furnace (No. 1), was dismantled and a new No. 1 built. The new No. 1 furnace (known for the first time as the Etowah Furnace) went into blast June 7, 1907. Dimensions of this stack were: height 78′, bosh 18′. Total annual capacity of the two furnaces was 150,000 tons of foundry iron which was sold under the brand name of "Etowah."

The Alabama Consolidated Coal and Iron Co. defaulted on its obligations and on April 26, 1913 all the company properties were acquired by the Alabama Company.

On Dec. 1, 1924 the Sloss-Sheffield Steel & Iron Co. acquired the two furnaces at Gadsden and renamed them the Sloss No. 9 and No. 10. The high cost of the ore and the transportation cost of fuel caused the furnaces to be abandoned between 1924 and 1926. The No. 10 was blown out in December 1924 and the No. 9 was blown out Sept. 30, 1926. Work of dismantling the stacks was begun in 1933 and completed in 1935.

This plant was equipped with a single strand Heyl & Patterson pig casting machine, the first one installed at a merchant furnace in Alabama.

FORT PAYNE FURNACE
Fort Payne, DeKalb County
Sept. 3, 1890

OF the many boom towns of the 1880's, Fort Payne is the best remembered. The Fort Payne Land and Improvement Co. purchased in 1886-7 some 36,000 acres in Wills Valley, DeKalb County. Fifty thousand shares of stock with a par value of $100 per share were issued. This stock was sold all over the country and the boom was cn.

On April 27, 1889 the Fort Payne Furnace Co. was organized with a capital of $200,000. It is said that every New England governor then in office held stock either in this project or the nearby Bay State Furnace Co. A prospectus of Fort Payne, published about 1890-91, contains the following statement:

> "At the Fort Payne Furnace an extensive body of rich brown ore is operated within 1,000 feet of the stock house, and the ore is dropped by means of a tramway into the stock house. This vein has been opened along the hillside for 1,500 feet. The red ore, soft and hard fossiliferous, abounds on the opposite side of the same ridge, and is carried to the furnaces at a minimum of cost. These veins of ore have been traced for miles, and contain sufficient quantities to last for generations."

The furnace was put into blast Sept. 3, 1890, the stack being 65' x 14'. It was soon discovered that the coal from the company property, (coked at the furnace in a battery of beehive ovens) did not coke satisfactorily. That circumstance and the low grade of the ores caused the furnace to operate at a loss, so that it was blown out sometime late in 1891. In 1893 the company went into the hands of a receiver and came under the control of the DeKalb Furnace Company which did not attempt to operate the plant. In 1895 the Bessemer Land and Improvement Co., with H. F. DeBardeleben as president, acquired both the Fort Payne and the Bay State Furnace at Fort Payne. DeBardeleben considered putting the Fort Payne into blast or moving it to Bessemer but this plan was abandoned and the furnace sold to a North Carolina company which dismantled it for scrap between 1898 and 1900.

Fort Payne Furnace, under construction in 1889.

First furnace built in Gadsden. Charcoal kilns are on the right, Coosa River in flood.

GADSDEN FURNACE
(Known also as Coosa Furnace, Quinn Furnace)
Gadsden, Etowah County
May 30, 1883

THE first blast furnace erected in the Gadsden district was the Gadsden Furnace of the Gadsden Iron Co. In 1881 the Crawfords of Indiana came South to select a location for an iron making operation and chose a site on the banks of the Coosa River within the limits of the City of Gadsden. Material for this furnace was salvaged from the dismantled Vigo Iron Co.'s stack No. 1 and shipped to Gadsden from Terre Haute, Ind. The furnace was 64′ high and 12′ in the bosh.

The plant went into blast on May 30, 1883 with an annual capacity of 8000 tons. A hot blast pipe stove preheated the air to about 900°. At the furnace were charcoal kilns, the wood for which was transported by river steamer. Brown hematite ore was bought from both Etowah and Cherokee Counties and red hematite was furnished from the vein near Attalla. A portion of the ore was transported by river and a portion via the Rome and Decatur Railroad. The plant was partially destroyed by fire in 1883 and rebuilt in 1884.

From that date until the Autumn of 1892 the plant operated more or less regularly. Sometime prior the Crawfords had sold an interest to Robert R. Kyle and J. M. Elliott, Jr. The Elliott Car Wheel Co. of Gadsden used a considerable portion of the output.

Apparently the furnace was not a low cost operation because it remained idle for ten years. In 1898 the Directory of the American Iron & Steel Institute lists the Coosa (Gadsden furnace) as "Abandoned." In 1901 the Southern Car & Foundry Co. bought the Gadsden Iron Co., revived the furnace and put it into blast in 1902. It operated for a part of 1903 and once again was blown out.

The Quinn Furnace Company was formed in 1905 and in January 1906 purchased the plant from the Southern Car & Foundry Co. The Quinn Company remodeled and slightly enlarged the stack to 65' x 12' and increased the capacity to 1800 tons a month. The furnace operated from the middle of 1906 until the Autumn of 1907, when it was blown out for the last time. Four years later, in 1911, the plant was dismantled.

HALE & MURDOCK FURNACE
(Known also as Wilson's Creek, Old Winston and Weston Furnace)
Lamar County, near Vernon
1859

IN 1859, when war clouds were already gathering, two New England-ers—Harrison Hale and Abraham Murdock—who had moved South to Columbus, Miss., built the first and only blast furnace ever erected in western Alabama.

Five years before they had erected a bloomery forge on Wilson's Creek about 2½ miles west of Vernon in the county of Fayette, later Sanford, and now Lamar County. In that same locality they built a small stone furnace. Cost of both imported and domestic iron was high, so they utilized the brown ore deposit near the town of Vernon, Alabama. Charcoal, the furnace fuel, they secured locally, burning it with slave labor. The usual line of small castings, hollow ware, plow points, horse shoes and other domestic implements were produced and hauled by wagon the 24 miles to Columbus, Miss.

The Hale and Murdock's Iron Co. charter was granted by the Alabama legislature in November 1862 with an authorized capital of $500,-000. The charter carries this addendum:

> "They having erected a blast furnace on Section 20, Township 15, Range 15 West, no spiritous liquor, in less than 5 gallon lots, is to be sold within 5 miles of said furnace."

During 1862 a new furnace was built under the direction of Joseph Weston, an experienced furnaceman, to replace the old one. This new plant went into blast early in 1863 and immediately began making small field ordnance under a contract with the Confederate government. In connection with the furnace was a forge. Size of the operation may be estimated from the fact that 150 men were employed. Much of the labor used not only in building but in operating the furnace was slave labor, the Confederate government supplying the skilled workmen.

It is said that General Nathan Bedford Forrest, C. S. A., had his horses shod here on his march to Corinth.

Because the furnace was off the beaten path, it escaped the Federal raiders and operated for about four years after the surrender. In January 1870 the company went out of business, largely because of the lack of transportation (25 miles from the railroad) and the competition of more favorably located furnaces. Last official notice of the Hale & Murdock's Iron Co. is an amendment, in 1871, to the company's charter allowing the sale of liquor within 2 miles of the then abandoned furnace.

An early photograph of Hattie Ensley Furnace with sand cast pig iron in the foreground.

HATTIE ENSLEY FURNACE
Sheffield, Colbert County
Dec. 31, 1887

THE Sheffield Land, Iron and Coal Co. promoted much of the City of Sheffield in Colbert County, Alabama. This company offered free certain tracts of lands on the Tennessee River to new enterprises. One such tract of twenty acres was deeded on Oct. 1, 1887 by the above to the Sheffield Furnace Co. A blast furnace was started in 1886 and on New Year's Eve, 1887, the first blast furnace in the City of Sheffield went into operation.

This stack, 75' x 17', was blown in on Pocahontas coke from Virginia and brown hematite ore from the adjoining county of Franklin. The plant was operated for only three months by the Sheffield Furnace Co. and then was sold to Enoch Ensley of Nashville, Tenn.

The Lady Ensley Coal, Iron & Railroad Co. was formed and on Jan. 28, 1891 the furnace was deeded by Ensley to that company. In that deed the property is first referred to as the "Hattie Ensley." The new company acquired considerable brown hematite land in adjoining Franklin County and also the Horse Creek Coal Mine (Big Seam) in

Walker County. A battery of 200 beehive coke ovens was built at the mine and the coke shipped to Sheffield.

Enoch Ensley died in 1891 and shortly afterward, during the Summer of 1892, the Hattie Ensley was blown out. The company was in financial trouble and on Nov. 18, 1893 the property was acquired for $70,000 by James P. Witherow of Pennsylvania, the original builder. The purchase price was credited to the claims of the Witherow Co.

In 1895 the plant was leased by the Colbert Furnace Co. which operated it infrequently until 1899. In that year the newly formed Sloss-Sheffield Steel & Iron Co. acquired a majority interest. It was not until April 6, 1903, however, that full title to the property was conveyed to the Sloss Company by a Chancery Court decree.

The furnace was rebuilt in 1900 and went into blast in 1901. The Hattie Ensley operated fairly regularly until it was blown out in 1916.

In 1915 a modern furnace, 81' x 18', was begun adjacent to the old hand filled Hattie Ensley No. 1. The new furnace (Sloss No. 5 or Hattie Ensley No. 2) went into blast during 1916. This stack used the stoves, blowing engines and boiler plant of the old furnace and thus cannot be considered as a separate blast furnace.

The old Hattie Ensley No. 1 was abandoned in 1916 but was not dismantled until 1926.

The new Hattie Ensley No. 2 continued to operate until 1926 when it was abandoned on account of unfavorable market and transportation factors. The stack was dismantled in 1931-32 at the same time the last Cole Furnace was dismantled.

The Hattie Ensley Furnace was without doubt the most successful of the North Alabama furnaces.

Holt Furnace, Tuscaloosa County. Photograph taken in 1925.

HOLT FURNACE
Holt, Tuscaloosa County
Aug. 1, 1903

IN the year 1899, nine small plants were producing practically all the sanitary pipe and fittings made in the United States. These plants were widely separated with units located in New York, Pennsylvania, Maryland, Indiana, Tennessee and three in Alabama at Anniston, Gadsden and Bessemer. In that year a group of Eastern business men conceived the plan of organizing a company to purchase these scattered units and consolidate them into a single enterprise, thus standardizing the industry. Pursuant to this plan the Central Foundry Company was formed and on April 1, 1899 took over the cast iron sanitary pipe business.

The Central Foundry Co. was a large consumer of both coke and pig iron. In an effort to avoid the fluctuations of the then rather unstable iron market the Central Foundry Co. decided to produce its own basic materials. To this end a new company, the Central Iron and Coal Co. was formed in 1901 for the purpose of erecting a blast furnace. The new company had the same officers as the Central Foundry Co. and was merely a subsidiary of the parent enterprise. A site for the blast furnace

was chosen in Tuscaloosa County a few miles north of the City of Tuscaloosa at Holt.

Construction of the blast furnace was begun in the latter part of 1901.
A battery of 164 beehive ovens was also built adjacent to the furnace
and went into operation in June, 1903. These ovens were constructed
to utilize the gas under the boilers and were among the first in the state
to be so equipped. The blast furnace went into blast Aug. 1, 1903 and
the first pig iron was cast on Aug. 3 of that year.

Coal land had been purchased at Kellerman, 16 miles from Holt.
Before the Kellerman Mine could be opened a railroad 13 miles long
had to be constructed to the property. This was done by the Mobile
and Ohio Railroad and the mine was opened late in 1903. Prior to that
coal had been obtained from the Tidewater Mine.

Ore property was bought near Woodstock on the AGS Railroad, midway between Bessemer and Tuscaloosa. This ore (brown hematite) was
the main source of supply during the entire history of the furnace operation. The Valley View Mine was opened on Red Mountain on a tract
of 107 acres at the head of 13th Street in Birmingham adjacent to the
land on which the cast iron statue of Vulcan now stands.

In 1909-10 a nodulizing plant was built for the preparation of pyrites
cinder from Spain. Later a contract was signed for the entire output of
pyrites cinder of the Virginia-Carolina Chemical Co.

The Central Iron and Coal Co. in 1902 contracted to build a battery
of 40 ten-ton Semet-Solvay by-product coke ovens. The new ovens were
completed in February 1904. This was the second such battery to be built
in the state. The Semet-Solvay Company, as stipulated in the contract,
leased and operated the plant for twenty years. A portion of the beehive
ovens continued to operate to supplement the by-product coke.

The original stack at Holt was 85' x 18' and rated at 150 tons. This
stack was in almost continuous operation from the date of blowing in,
being relined eight times in nine years. In 1912 a new stack was built,
the height being the same, 85' with the bosh widened to 19'. This new
furnace went into blast Dec. 4, 1912 with an annual rating of 72,000 tons.
At the same time the new stack was being built an additional battery of
20 Semet-Solvay by-product coke ovens (12 ton) were added to the
original 40. Following completion of these ovens, all the coke was produced in the by-product ovens, the beehive ovens being discontinued.

The product of the blast furnace at Holt was used both for company
consumption and as merchant iron. In 1907 a soil pipe plant had been
built at Holt and in 1912 a very large plant was constructed there to

replace the older one. The Central Foundry Company, however, rarely used more than 40% of the furnace make, the balance being offered on the open market. This iron was sold under the brand names, Warrior and Tuscaloosa; the former a high manganese iron and the latter straight foundry iron.

In 1924 the Valley View mine ceased to operate. Even prior to that, the Central Company had purchased various ores from the Sloss Company, the Alabama Company and the Woodward Company. On Aug. 19, 1929 the Holt Furnace was blown out. The Kellerman Mine and the by-product ovens continued to operate until 1932.

During the early part of 1940, the Central Iron and Coal Company went into general equity receivership. On Sept. 4, 1940 the Holt Furnace and by-product plant at Holt and the Kellerman Coal Mines and the brown ore mines at Giles, Ala. were sold in Federal Court to the Associated Metals & Mineral Corporation of New York City, whose attorney announced that "efforts will be made to operate the properties instead of 'junking' them as has been erroneously reported."

Ironaton Furnace No. 1, Talladega County. View taken about 1908.

IRONATON FURNACES
(Known also as Clifton Furnaces)
Talladega County, near Talladega
No. 1—April 16, 1885
No. 2—July 1891

THE Clifton Iron Co. was incorporated in 1880 with a capital of
$300,000, most of which was subscribed by Samuel Noble and his
brothers. Horace Ware put up certain ore lands which he had bought
just after the Civil War. At a place nine miles east of the town of
Talladega and in the County of Talladega, they built a charcoal furnace.
The stack, 55' x 12', was blown in April 16, 1885. The brown hematite
ore was obtained immediately behind the furnace and taken to the stock
house on trams. The charcoal was also obtained in the vicinity. Daily
capacity of the furnace was 40 tons of "high grade foundry and car wheel
pig iron."

In 1881 the Clifton Iron Co. acquired the Alabama Iron Co., owners
of the Jenifer Furnace. When the furnace at Ironaton was completed a
railroad was built to connect the two plants. Another railroad, now a
part of the L & N, was built to Sylacauga which served the Ironaton

plant. In 1889 the Clifton Iron Co. sold the Jenifer Furnace property to the Jenifer Iron Co. leaving the Ironaton plant as the Clifton Iron Company's only furnace operation. During 1891 a second and larger charcoal furnace, 60' x 14', was blown in at Ironaton. The combined capacity of the two stacks was 33,000 tons annually.

It became apparent that the excessive cost of fuel was making charcoal iron almost prohibitive and as a result the No. 1 furnace was remodeled (the bosh being increased to 13') and converted to a coke furnace in 1895. The coke was purchased in the Birmingham district and shipped by the L & N to Ironaton.

The Ironaton plant was acquired by the Alabama Consolidated Coal and Iron Co. in 1899 at the time of its organization. A year later the No. 2 furnace, which had been idle since 1895, was remodeled, enlarged to 67' x 15' and converted to a coke furnace. The coke for Ironaton was obtained from the Lewisburg Coal Mines owned by the Alabama Consolidated Coal and Iron Co.

In 1913 the Alabama Consolidated Coal and Iron Co. failed and a new corporation, the Alabama Company, absorbed the properties. At this time the two furnaces at Ironaton had a combined capacity of 130,000 tons annually, both having been rebuilt, the No. 1, 70' x 17-1/6', and the No. 2, 76' x 16'. A skip incline had been added to the No. 1 in 1897 but the No. 2 remained a hand filled furnace.

The Sloss-Sheffield Steel and Iron Co. acquired the Alabama Company Dec. 1, 1924, the furnaces having been blown out earlier in the year. These furnaces were abandoned in 1925 and dismantled between 1925 and 1929.

Both the charcoal and the coke iron at the Ironaton Furnaces was sold under the brand name of "Clifton."

Woodcut made from photograph taken of Irondale Furnace in 1873. Note wooden trestle over Shades Creek in foreground.

IRONDALE FURNACE

(Known also as Cahawba Iron Works, McKee Furnace)
Jefferson County, near Birmingham
Dec. 1863 or Jan. 1864

ON April 6, 1862 the Battle of Shiloh began and the following day the Confederate retreat started Northward. Northwest Mississippi came under the dominance of the Union Army. At Holly Springs, Mississippi, Jones-McElwain and Co. had a foundry at which ordnance was cast for the Confederate Government but after the Battle of Corinth, in the Autumn of 1862 it became clear that the Holly Springs Iron Works were doomed. The machinery was therefore sold to the Confederate Ordnance Department and a large portion of it was shipped to the arsenal at Macon, Ga.

With the capital derived from this sale and with an advance made by the Confederate Government, Jones and McElwain purchased land in upper Shades Valley on Shades Creek in Jefferson County. W. S. McElwain was the practical iron-master of the company and he chose the site of the proposed furnace. The work of building a stone, charcoal furnace was begun in the Spring of 1863.

The following is a letter of this period written to A. T. Jones, President of the Shelby Iron Co.:

> "Office Cahawba Iron Works,
> Jefferson County, Elyton P. O., Ala.
> May 20, 1863.
>
> Dear Sir:
> Some days since your Mr. Edwards* was here and said your Company would like to get some gas pipe and furnish me with iron for ties for my stack, upon same terms as old prices, enclosed sizes I hand you of the Iron I now require.
> Yours truly,
> W. S. McElwain."

The trade was made on the basis of 1 foot of $1\frac{1}{4}''$ pipe to 4 pounds of iron.

The Irondale furnace was about 41' high and $10\frac{1}{2}'$ in the bosh. Its stack apparently differed slightly from others of that era in that it was constructed of heavy masonry at the base and of brick, banded with iron ties on the mantle. There is no accurate record of the exact date on which the furnace was blown in but it is known that the plant was in operation either in December of 1863 or January of 1864.

Output of the furnace (about 6 or 7 tons a day) was contracted for by the Nitre and Mining Bureau. The iron was hauled by ox cart or mule team down the Montevallo Road to Brock's Gap and there delivered to the Selma, Rome and Dalton Railroad and taken to the Confederate arsenal at Selma.

During the Civil War two furnaces of Jefferson County made pig iron from the red hematite of Red Mountain. The Irondale furnace used the "soft" ore of the Helen Bess mine. The so-called "soft ore" was the ore near the surface which had been leached out by the weather to a depth of 50 to 100 feet. A small tramway was built from the mine (located on the Eastern slope of Red Mountain) to the furnace, a distance of about three miles.

Some time in the Spring or early Summer of 1864 the first successful coke iron made in Alabama was produced at the Irondale furnace. The following is an extract from a report written July 15, 1864 by Maj. Wm. R. Hunt, officer in command at Selma, to Col. J. M. St. John, Chief of Nitre and Mining Bureau in Richmond, Va.:

> "Iron Ore, Coal and Limestone, the three necessaries to produce pig iron, lie in contiguity in this State and in unlimited quantities; in many places they approach within half a mile of each other, these presenting to the Iron Master unusual facilities.

---

*See Edwards Furnace.

"Mr. McElwain has at my request tried the experiment of manufacturing iron with coke, in a blast furnace. His furnace was not built for Coke being only about 40 feet high, and using cold instead of hot blast. Yet notwithstanding these disadvantages, his experiment is very satisfactory, his yield was increased from 7 to 10 tons per day, and the iron produced was peculiarly fitted for rolling mill purposes."

The experiment was not tried again in Alabama for twelve years. Like all the rest of the iron-masters of that age, McElwain used a large number of slaves hired by the year from their masters. Many slave holders, fleeing before the Union Army, were glad to lease their slaves in Alabama. The following letter, to Wm. P. Browne, written after the surrender, is evidence:

> "Leedstown, Va.
> Nov. 5, 1865
>
> Dear Sir:
> Can you tell me what has become of McElwain & Co. and whether there is any possibility of my getting anything from them for the hire of my negroes at their Iron Works.
> I hold his bonds for a very considerable amount.
> Sgd. Wm. Witt."

Gen. Wilson of the Federal Cavalry marched through Jones Valley toward Elyton to reunite his forces with Croxton. Sometime about the middle of March, 1865, these Union raiders came upon the "Cahawba Iron Works" at Irondale and set fire to all the wooden superstructure of the plant.

At a time when the entire Southland was struggling to adjust itself to the bitterness of defeat, McElwain was seeking Northern capital to rebuild his plant. This he found in Ohio and a new company, the Jefferson Iron Company, was formed. Immediately McElwain set to work repairing the damage done by the Union raiders. The height of the furnace was increased to 46 feet and hot blast pipe stoves were installed. A steam blowing engine was substituted for the ineffective water powered blower. The rebuilt plant went into blast late in 1865 or early in 1866. About 500 men were required to keep the furnace supplied with charcoal and ore, run the machine shop and foundry and maintain the plant. The scarcity of money may be judged from the fact that McElwain was able to contract for 100,000 cords of wood at 75c per cord.

For a time the furnace prospered, making domestic and agricultural implements and equipment for the railroads. Only three furnaces in the

Remains of Irondale Furnace in Jefferson County, showing condition about 1893.

state were in blast in 1866; Bibb (or Strother), Hale and Murdock, and Irondale. Within a few years, however, other plants more favorably situated went into blast and Irondale began to lose money. Timber became harder to obtain and its cost higher. The high transportation cost (amounting to $2.00 a ton to the railhead) also put the plant at a disadvantage.

McKee, Fuller & Co. of Pennsylvania in 1871 leased the furnace for 10 years and after making some repairs and improvements put the plant into operation. Within a year, however, the plant was re-leased to James Thomas & Co. also of Pennsylvania. The panic of 1873 caused the blowing out of the furnace. In 1876 the boilers were sold to the Eureka Company and hauled to Oxmoor by eight span of oxen. A little later the blowing engine was moved to Woodstock and was used at the Edwards furnace.

The old Irondale furnace is now but a heap of stone and brick, almost unknown and unvisited.

JANNEY FURNACE
Calhoun County, near Ohatchee
Destroyed 1864

ON Jan. 1, 1863 Abraham Lincoln issued the Emancipation Proclamation. The Battle of Gettysburg was fought that year and the star of the Confederacy began to set. The armies of the North were pushing deeper and deeper into the Southland.

In that time of despair, in the face of adverse conditions, one of the most pretentious of Alabama's stone furnaces was begun, whether from the motive of patriotism or profit it is impossible to judge, but a certain amount of courage was necessary to embark on any venture at that time.

A. A. Janney had been in the foundry business in Montgomery for many years prior to the war. It is a matter of record that he had used much iron from the Cane Creek furnace. It was natural, therefore, that he should seek near Cane Creek for a location on which to build a furnace. The site he chose was within two miles of the Coosa River and not over five miles from the Cane Creek furnace.

Slaves, whose masters were refugeeing before the advancing Union armies, built at least two of the furnaces of that period. A Dr. Smith of Tennessee brought 200 hands South with him to keep the Federal soldiers from freeing them. These he hired to Janney for the purpose of building his furnace.

First a portion of the hill was cut away and a retaining wall built. Behind that, and even with the top of the stack another plot was leveled off to serve as a stocking yard. Huge stones, many of which weighed more than a ton, were slowly shaped by hand and put into place. The stack stood 50′ high and measured 11′ across the bosh. On the east side of the furnace a reservoir was built into which water was pumped from the creek. Between the furnace and the reservoir was a bank, 25 to 30′ high, on which was the foundation for the blowing engines and probably the boilers. All such machinery was made by Janney at his foundry and shipped up the Coosa River to the landing a few miles away.

The hill against which the furnace was built contained sufficient pockets of brown ore to operate the furnace for some time, in fact, a little of this ore is still being mined on a small scale. The woods were largely uncut and could have furnished charcoal for many years.

It is on record that the superstructure of the plant and all other wooden appurtenances were destroyed by Gen. Lovell H. Rousseau on

Janney Furnace in Calhoun County, destroyed in 1864 by Union raiders.

July 14, 1864. There is, however, a controversial issue regarding this furnace. Some claim that the plant operated and some that it did not. However the lining of the stack is not blackened by fire but at one time it may have been lined with brick. There is no slag on the ground to indicate even one run and not a trace of charcoal anywhere.

Remains of the furnace are still standing. They are among the best preserved in the state and a tribute to the workmanship of those old slave stone-cutters.

JENIFER FURNACE
(Known also as Salt Creek and Alabama Furnace)
Talladega County, near Munford
1863

FOR one moment the battle flag of the Confederacy broke through the Union lines at Gettysburg, faltered and fell back. The turning point had come. That July afternoon in 1863 marked the beginning of the end of the Confederacy. The industrially poor South needed desperately cannon and arms for the Army of the Potomac, the Army of the West.

On January 23, of this same year the firm of Clabaugh and Curry had purchased for $2,940 lands on Salt Creek, some two miles from the little town of Munford. On this property the firm began the building with slave labor of a stone furnace—the first in Talladega County. Clabaugh, the brother-in-law of Horace Ware, iron-master of Shelby, was the practical furnaceman of the venture. The furnace went into blast that same year. J. A. Curry's interest, however, was purchased by Samuel Clabaugh on Nov. 11, 1863 and the firm became Clabaugh and Co. A portion of the capital needed to build the plant was advanced by the Confederate Government and this money was repaid in pig iron. In common with the other iron manufacturers of the Civil War era the plant was operated under a contract with the Nitre and Mining Bureau which detailed skilled men from the Army.

The brown ore was mined by slaves from open pits within a mile of the furnace. The surrounding forests were cut and burned in dust pits to supply the charcoal. The little furnace did not produce over 5 or 6 tons a day and this was hauled to the Selma, Rome and Dalton Railroad and shipped to the arsenal at Selma.

Most authorities state that the furnace was destroyed by Federal raiders in 1864 but there is conclusive evidence that the plant remained in operation for the duration of the Civil War. The following from the Alabama Reporter of Talladega, is dated April 27, 1865:

> "The iron establishment of Clabaugh and Curry was destroyed, as were the other iron establishments in the neighborhood of Oxford, Calhoun County, Ala. The Yankees left our town Sunday morning and moved in the direction of Oxford."

The war had laid waste the entire southland; of food there was little, of money there was practically none. Samuel Clabaugh put up a one-half interest in the Salt Creek Iron Works to secure a mere $700 note; and a one-quarter interest in the property was sold for $1500.

Jenifer Furnace, Talladega County, as it appeared in 1901.

The section of land on which the furnace stood was sold at public sale, Oct. 25, 1869 for $3144.50. On Dec. 31, 1869 the property was resold to Horace Ware, the builder of Shelby who had begun to purchase other lands in his own name. In 1870 Samuel Clabaugh sold his remaining interest for $25,000 and Ware was ready to begin operating. He felt, however, that he was not capable of financing the whole operation and called on his friend Stephen S. Glidden of Ohio.

On Nov. 2, 1872 Ware and Glidden organized the Alabama Iron Company with a capital of $80,000. S. S. Glidden subscribed to 600 shares and Horace Ware to 200 shares. On Dec. 22, 1873 the capital stock was increased to $100,000, Glidden taking 100 shares, Samuel Bayard 80 shares and James L. Orr 20 shares.

A new furnace was begun on the site of the old one. This new stack was 41' high and 8'-8" across the bosh, "open top with bonnet." The furnace was built of stone, the bottom portion of which was the frustrum of a pyramid, the top being round. *This was the last stone furnace erected in Alabama.*

This furnace was put into blast Oct. 1, 1873. An interesting letter from Stephen Glidden, the manager, to John T. Milner giving some interesting sidelights on its production and operating cost, recites that the average output for 1873-4 was 19.3 tons a day. Ore was delivered to the furnace at $1.50 a ton, charcoal at $1.08 a bu. The total cost of raw materials was $12.15, and labor $1.50 per ton of iron.

Glidden hired convicts from the state and he seems to have been the only operator to use them as furnace hands. This practice was abandoned however, in 1881 when the property was sold.

The Alabama Iron Company was bought, Dec. 1, 1881 by the Clifton Iron Company for $150,000. Samuel Noble, one of the officials of the Clifton Company, renamed the plant Jenifer in honor of his mother, Jenifer Ward Noble. The furnace was remodeled in 1884 to 55' x 10'.

On June 28, 1889 the Jenifer Iron Company was organized with capital of $100,000, the following stock being subscribed: John Ward Noble—350 shares; William Noble—350 shares; George Noble—250 shares; George Abbott Noble—50 shares.

In 1892 the furnace was completely rebuilt, the old stone stack being dismantled and a new iron stack 56' x 11' built. Jenifer was not only the last stone furnace *built* in Alabama but was also the last one *operated* in Alabama.

Shortly afterward on Nov. 15, 1894, another Noble, nephew of J. W. Noble, bought the property and formed the Jenifer Furnace Company.

The plant was idle a good portion of the time due to the decrease in demand for charcoal iron.

In 1901 the furnace was rebuilt and converted from charcoal to coke. The new furnace was 75' x 15'. The Weller Coal Mine in Jefferson County was bought and 100 beehive ovens erected.

During the slack market of 1903 the furnace was blown out and remained idle until the World War created a demand for iron.

For a time the property was known as the Jenifer Coal and Iron Co., then the Central Alabama Coal and Iron Co., and during the World War was operated as the Thomas Furnace Co. In 1921 the entire property was purchased by W. Aubrey Thomas of Ohio and is now the Jenifer Iron Co.

The furnace was blown out Nov. 11, 1920 due to the high cost of fuel transportation. The last carload of iron from this historic plant was shipped on May 3, 1921. In the Spring of 1939 the work of dismantling the plant was begun, thus ending the story of an operation that had been in existence for more than three-quarters of a century.

KNIGHT FURNACE

(Known also as Choccolocco Iron Works)
Talladega County, near Munford
1863 or 1864

J. L. and W. C. Orr together with Samuel Hunter bought in 1854 the property of a Mr. Bagby, "twelve miles northeast of Talladega, on Choccolocco Creek, on which they have erected a large and capacious building, and have procured all the machinery that can be profitably used in manufacturing Cotton Gins."

The Orr brothers died just after the Civil War began. The administrator of the estate sold on March 11, 1863 the lands and the mill to Jacob B. and Benjamin Knight for $20,000. It is said that the Knight brothers refugeed from New Orleans after the surrender of that city in 1862, bringing with them a number of slaves and considerable cash. The gin manufactory was converted into a cotton spinning mill.

Shortly after the purchase of the gin manufactory, the Knight brothers began the erection of a stone furnace. The site they chose was directly across Choccolocco Creek from the cotton mill and about 75 yards below the mill dam. The Confederate Government supplied a portion of the capital which was to be repaid in pig iron. The finished iron necessary to construct the furnace had to be requisitioned through the Nitre and Mining Bureau. The following letter illustrates this rigid control:

> "Choccolocco Iron Works,
> Talladega County, Ala.
> July 13, 1863
>
> Maj. W. R. Hunt, In Charge Iron & Mining,
> Selma, Alabama
> We require at our works 2 wrought iron plates 15″ wide ⅜ thick and 5 ft. long. Iron sufficient for 24 cooling shovels.
> Very respectfully,
> J. B. Knight & Co."

This bill of iron was authorized to be supplied by the Shelby Iron Co.

The furnace was located two and one-half miles northwest of the town of Munford and three and one-fourth miles due west of the Salt Creek Iron Works. The stack was approximately 30′ x 7′ and lined with brick made within one-half mile of the furnace site. The little plant went into operation early in 1864 or possibly during the last days of 1863. The daily capacity was between 5 and 7 tons of cold blast pig iron.

Ore was obtained in part from small brown hematite deposits near the plant and in part from ore beds east of the Salt Creek furnace, about four miles distant. Ore and charcoal were hauled by teams to the bank directly behind the furnace, the bank having been cut away to make a level storage yard.

The usual line of domestic and agricultural implements was cast here. As was common practice of that day a semi-forge operated in connection with the furnace to produce such articles as hinges, tire iron, etc.

The Selma, Rome and Dalton Railroad was already in operation as far as Blue Mountain near the present site of Anniston. This line ran within three miles of the furnace and the bulk of the iron made here was hauled by teams to this railroad and transhipped to the arsenal at Selma.

It is known that the cotton mill and furnace were destroyed by Federal raiders and it is supposed that this was done at the same time the Salt Creek Iron Works was burned, sometime late in April of 1865. That the Yankee raiders did a thorough job of destroying may be judged by the fact that the public sale of the Knight property in 1869 brought exactly $303.00.

Today the remains of the old dam may be seen and below that on the east bank of Choccolocco Creek a heap of stones which mark the furnace site.

LADY ENSLEY FURNACE
Sheffield, Colbert County
April 25, 1889

IN 1888 Enoch Ensley of Nashville, Tenn., who had recently sold his interests in the Birmingham District, took his capital to North Alabama and formed the Lady Ensley Furnace Co. He was deeded a twenty acre tract on the Tennessee River on May 21, 1888 by the Sheffield Land, Iron and Coal Co. with the stipulation that a blast furnace be erected thereon. This property adjoined that of the "Hattie Ensley" Furnace in the City of Sheffield, Colbert County. On this site the Lady Ensley furnace was erected and was blown in April 25, 1889. The stack was 75' x 17' and was rated at 30,000 gross tons annually. The ore (brown hematite) was procured from the Ensley mines in Franklin County and the coke from the Pocahontas field in Virginia. Shortly after the furnace went into blast, the Horse Creek Coal Mine on the Big Seam in Walker County (now Dora) was acquired and 200 beehive coke ovens were built there.

Enoch Ensley died in 1891 and the company went into the hands of a receiver. In June 1892 the furnace was blown out and remained idle until 1901. On May 18, 1900 the property was deeded to the North Alabama Furnace Co. in which the Sloss-Sheffield Steel & Iron Co. had acquired a 2/3 interest thereby coming into control of the operation.

In 1900-01 the furnace was rebuilt but not enlarged and was blown in during the summer of 1901. In 1906 the plant was remodeled and the annual capacity increased to 70,000 tons. The Lady Ensley operated until 1910 and then was blown out. In 1916 the furnace was dismantled.

Product of the Lady Ensley was foundry and forge pig iron, most of which was shipped North to points on the Ohio River.

Little Cahaba Furnace No. 2, built about 1863, adjacent to No. 1
Furnace in Bibb County.

LITTLE CAHABA FURNACE
(Known also as Brighthope Furnace and Browne's Dam Furnace)
On Little Cahaba River, Bibb County
Little Cahaba No. 1 About 1848
Little Cahaba No. 2 About 1863

HISTORY of the Little Cahaba Iron Works is largely lost in the mists of the past. One of the oldest furnaces of the state, it is nevertheless one which has left little authentic data on its operations. It is a matter of record, however, that on Sept. 2, 1846 William Phineas Browne entered land in Bibb County as "SW¼ SW¼ of Sec. 13, Township 24, Range 10 East," on which the furnace was built. Later Browne entered more land surrounding this area on which were small surface deposits of brown hematite ore and an abundance of wood for charcoal.

About 1848 a stone furnace stack was built on the north bank of the Little Cahaba River. Upstream about 150 yards a dam was constructed and a flume built to the furnace to supply the power for the blowing tubs. Behind the stack was a hill and a wooden trestle connected the two for the purpose of charging the furnace. It is known that Wm. P. Browne built the dam in 1847 but definite proof as to when the furnace went into operation is lacking.

Browne himself was not an iron-master; he was one of the original owners and operators of the Montevallo Coal Mines. It is most probable that J. Newton Smith, a local iron-master, was his partner. A letter written to Browne, dated Nov. 12, 1853, signed by P. Webb, says in part: "I have left at the furnace some 1200 or 1500 pounds of the *oar* which I hope you have tested more effectually. It is high time we should know the value of the *oar*." From this letter it is evident that the furnace was in blast prior to that date.

It is probable that this furnace was idle for a long period prior to the Civil War. J. P. Lesley in his directory of 1858 lists a forge on the Little Cahaba River but makes no mention of a blast furnace. Sometime during the Civil War, however, the property was leased by W. L. Ward and Co. and a contract was signed with the Confederate Government. A second and larger stack was built within a few yards of the older furnace and this is listed by the Nitre and Mining Bureau as being in blast in 1864. This same report indicates that Ward operated a forge in connection with the furnace. Output of this furnace was probably shipped to the Confederate Arsenal at Selma.

Among the papers of William P. Browne who owned the land on which the "iron works" stood, was found the original plans of the little stone stack. These gave the total height of the furnace as 20', bosh 8'-10½", hearth 2'. The second and larger stack was about 29' high and 7½' in the bosh.

Available evidence indicates that the Little Cahaba Iron Works was destroyed by Gen. Wilson at the same time the Bibb Iron Works was burned in April 1865. Until a very few years ago these furnace remains were the best preserved in the state. For many years after the plant had been abandoned the old forge hammer could be seen at the furnace site. Quite recently, however, the old stones were moved away by a saw mill operator for use as a boiler setting and the last trace of this early iron maker was virtually destroyed.

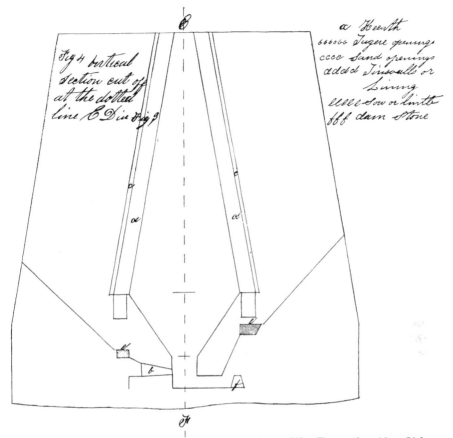

Original plan of first Little Cahaba Furnace, drawn about 1846. This is the oldest Alabama blast furnace plan known to exist.

MARY PRATT FURNACE
Birmingham, Jefferson County
April 1883

IN 1882 H. F. DeBardeleben and W. T. Underwood began erection of the Mary Pratt furnace—the third to be built in Birmingham—on a tract purchased from the Elyton Land Company. The property bordered on First Avenue and lay between the present Sloss City furnaces and the Avondale Mills in Birmingham.

The Mary Pratt Furnace Company was incorporated on March 29, 1883 with a capitalization of $300,000. The furnace was blown in April 1883. The little stack was 55' high and 11' in the bosh. The Directory of American Iron and Steel Association of 1884 states:

> "Cold, warm or hot blast; fuel; sometimes coke and sometimes charcoal depending on the requirements of the iron market."

The Mary Pratt was rated at 15,000 tons annually of foundry iron.

Furnace coke was supplied by the Pratt Coal and Coke Co. and the ore (red hematite) was bought from local mining contractors and at first came from near McCalla, south of Bessemer. Brown ore was also bought from East Alabama as well as Jefferson and Tuscaloosa counties. Somewhat later land was leased on Red Mountain from the Alice Furnace Company. Development of this property was a contributing factor in the building of the Birmingham Mineral Railroad.

The Mary Pratt operated rather steadily during the good business years of the 80's. Early in 1889 the furnace was blown out, rebuilt, and enlarged to 65' x 14' for the use of coke and its capacity increased to 20,000 tons. A little later it was rated at 30,000 tons. The furnace was blown in late in 1889 and operated until the panic of 1893 when it was again blown out and remained idle much of the time thereafter.

In 1898 the Mary Pratt Furnace Co. was sold by court decree at public auction for $35,000. A year later the property was acquired by the Alabama Consolidated Coal and Iron Company and the furnace was overhauled preparatory to being blown in. For some reason the plans were changed and the plant continued to stand idle. In 1903 the Mary Pratt property was sold to the Alabama Great Southern Railroad for a storage yard and in 1903-4 the Mary Pratt furnace was dismantled.

The Mary Pratt is an excellent example of the fair weather furnace which had no permanent source of raw materials and operated only during times of great pig iron demand.

Mary Pratt Furnace, Birmingham. Picture taken about 1890.

MONTGOMERY FURNACE
Montgomery County, near Montgomery
Begun 1887

IN 1887 the Montgomery Furnace and Chemical Company began the erection of a charcoal blast furnace. Like three other plants in this state, the Montgomery furnace was destined never to operate.

From the Iron Age of Dec. 1, 1887, is the following extract:

"Montgomery, Ala., 42 (Charcoal kilns of the Pierce process) kilns building by the Montgomery Furnace and Chemical Company, having a capital of $400,000. This company is also building a charcoal furnace under the charge of Dr. Dennis Church. It is 60 feet high by 12 feet bosh, with two iron hot-blast stoves, having thirty-two 12 foot pipes. The bulk of the alcohol plant is finished, the casting-house of the furnace is nearly built, the foundations are in, the columns and ring are up. The furnace is to have a capacity of 50 tons, and it is expected to be in running order on June 1, 1888. The wood is to come from the Alabama River, on which the plant is located, while the ores are to be brought 35 miles from the brown ore belt of East Alabama. One of the principal grounds for its location at the point mentioned has been that the iron can be shipped by navigation to the seaboard."

Work on the furnace was suspended shortly after this article appeared and the furnace remained in an uncompleted state until about 1895 when it was dismantled.

NORTH ALABAMA FURNACE
Florence, Lauderdale County
Oct. 1889

THE Florence Land, Mining and Manufacturing Co. was incorporated with a capital of $800,000 by a group of Florence Citizens on Aug. 31, 1886. The company purchased thousands of acres in and near the city of Florence and set about the task of bringing industries to North Alabama.

On Jan. 21, 1887 the Florence Land Company contracted to give certain lands to the Florence Coal, Coke & Iron Co. provided the latter build a blast furnace within a certain stipulated time. The furnace was begun but for some reason was abandoned after a short time and the contract was annulled and cancelled.

With a stated capital of $2,000,000, the North Alabama Furnace, Foundry and Land Company was incorporated April 28, 1887. A portion of the capital was raised in New York and Ohio and part in the South.

On Oct. 1, 1887 the Florence Land Co. drew up articles of agreement with the North Alabama Company similar to the contract cancelled with the Florence Coal, Coke & Iron Co. From that document is this extract:

> "The said Furnace Company will at once take charge of the furnace commenced under said agreement together with the 25 acres of land appertaining thereto, including all material and machinery thereto belonging, and will continue the erection of said furnace (being a 100 ton furnace) so as to have the same completed by Sept. 1, 1888."

As an inducement or reward, the Florence Land Co. placed in the hands of a Trustee for the North Alabama Company 300 town lots, 1,000 acres of ore land in Tennessee, and the 25 acre furnace site located in Florence and on the Tennessee River.

The North Alabama Company built a brick yard at the furnace capable of making 14,000 brick a day and began the work of completing the plant.

The furnace, which should have been in operation on or before September 1, 1888, was not put into blast until October 1889 or more than a year later. The various lands held by the Trustee were nevertheless assigned to the North Alabama Company as soon as the plant went into blast.

This furnace was 75′ x 16′ and was rated at 30,000 tons a year. A large portion of its output, like that of other furnaces in this district, was shipped by river to Northern markets for general foundry purposes. The brown hematite ore was mined from Wayne County, Tenn. and shipped the 20 miles by rail to the furnace. Coke was purchased from both Virginia and Alabama.

In little more than a year (Feb. 28, 1891) the North Alabama Furnace, Foundry and Land Co. was in the courts. On Nov. 23, 1892, a court sale was ordered and on March 31, 1893 the property was bid in by the Spathite Iron Co. for the sum of $69,551.37. The furnace, which had been idle since July 1, 1890, was rebuilt in 1893 (bosh decreased to 14′) and went into blast early in 1894.

The Spathite Iron Co., a Tennessee concern, mined Spathite Ore (not Spathic) from Iron City in Lawrence County, Tenn., and also some brown ore. The fuel was coke, shipped from Pineville, Ky. From the Geological Survey of 1896 is the following comment: "Spathic iron made only at Florence . . . This iron commands $.50 to $1.00 more per ton than pig."

Apparently the Spathic iron was not a success because on Nov. 25, 1895 the Louisville Banking Co. of Louisville, Ky. had to take over the property. The plant had remained idle since the Spring of 1895 and was finally dismantled in 1901.

OXFORD FURNACE
Calhoun County, near Anniston
April 1863

AS early as 1848-9 the first state geologist, Michael Toumey, said of the land around the present town of Anniston:

"The vicinity of a bold stream, abundance of fuel, excellent building material and proximity to a railroad, point to this locality as the site of one of the future great iron manufacturing establishments of the state."

It was not until 1862, however, that Toumey's prophecy was partially realized. During that second year of the Civil War the Oxford Iron Co. was organized with a capital of $24,000, most of which was local. The Confederate Government advanced a portion of the money to build the plant and also detailed skilled men from the army to assist in construction and operation.

The furnace was 45′ high and 9′ across the bosh, constructed of stone along the conventional lines of that era. It was put into blast during April of 1863.

Strangely enough there is a connection between this plant and the first blast furnace in the South to manufacture coke iron. The East Tennessee Iron Co. built a furnace near Chattanooga and in 1860 produced about 500 tons of coke iron. Due to various causes that plant was dismantled and a portion of the machinery was brought to Oxford in 1862 by Giles Edwards.

Ore for this furnace (brown hematite) was obtained within a quarter mile of the plant and hauled there by teams. Pine forests surrounding the plant furnished an abundance of wood for charcoal. As was the case with almost all the iron-makers of that time, the labor was performed by hired slaves and skilled workmen detailed from the Confederate Army.

The Oxford Iron Company was under contract with the Confederate Government to supply a certain tonnage per month. A large part of this metal was shipped to the arsenal at Selma via the Selma, Rome and Dalton Railroad.

During the latter part of April, 1865, a detachment of Gen. Croxton's command marched through the town of Talladega, "destroyed the iron works of Clabaugh and Curry and departed in the direction of Oxford." It was on this raid that Croxton, marching to rejoin Gen. Wilson in Geogia, came upon and burned the Oxford furnace.

The Oxford Iron Co. was never revived but the property was sold in 1871 to Samuel Noble. On this land the Woodstock Iron Co. was built and old Michael Toumey's prophecy came true for "here was built one of the great iron manufacturing establishments of the state."

Oxmoor furnaces in 1873 after being rebuilt. Note cylindrical iron furnace tops on stone base at left center of this early woodcut.

OXMOOR FURNACES
Jefferson County, near Birmingham
No. 1—Oct. or Nov. 1863
No. 2—Oct. or Nov. 1873

SHORTLY after outbreak of the Civil War, the Alabama Arms Manufacturing Co. was organized for the purpose of mining ore and manufacturing iron for Confederate ordnance. Incorporators of this company did not have sufficient capital to develop their mineral property and two of their number were delegated to petition the Confederate Government for financial aid. A large portion of the necessary money was advanced by the Confederacy with the stipulation that the advance be repaid in pig iron.

The Red Mountain Iron and Coal Company, with a capital of $1,250,000, was incorporated Nov. 5, 1862, "a corporation successor to the Alabama Arms Manufacturing Co." This new company began erection of two stone blast furnaces under the direction of Wm. McClane. Only one of these furnaces was completed and about one year later, in the late Fall of 1863, the first blast furnace of Jefferson County was put into operation. Shortly afterward, T. M. Brannan became superintendent and Moses Stroup (of Round Mountain and Tannehill) was put in charge of the charcoal burning.

Due to the company's contract with the Nitre and Mining Bureau of the Confederate States, a very large portion of its product was shipped via the Selma, Rome & Dalton Railroad to the C. S. A. arsenal at Selma. A certain portion of the output was consigned to the arsenal at Rome, Ga. Ore for this furnace came from Red Mountain and was hauled by teams the short distance to the plant. As was common practice in other furnaces of that time, charcoal from surrounding forests was the fuel used.

The little Oxmoor furnace stood about 32' high and was 9' or 10' in the bosh. Considering the size of the stack and the highly silicious content of the red hematite ore (soft) it is doubtful whether the daily capacity of the furnace ever exceeded five or six tons. In order to produce this amount of iron, not less than 60 men were required at the furnace and between 200 and 300 slaves for cutting and hauling wood for the charcoal burners.

Early in 1865 Gen. Wilson of the Federal Army concentrated a force of picked cavalry in North Alabama. The purpose was a series of raids through Central Alabama to culminate in the capture and destruction of the Confederate arsenal at Selma. Wilson divided his command and the two divisions marched by different routes toward the town of Elyton in Jones Valley. At that place the forces were reunited during the last of March. Once again Wilson divided his command, Croxton going south in the direction of Tuscaloosa and Wilson taking the Valley Road to the east. On March 30 the detachment under Wilson came upon the furnace of the Red Mountain Iron and Coal Co. and burned all the wooden buildings and destroyed the machinery.

The plant remained in a wrecked condition until sometime in 1872 when the Eureka Mining and Transportation Co. was organized to take over the old Red Mountain Company. Daniel Pratt, a wealthy cotton gin manufacturer from South Alabama, supplied a considerable portion of the capital. The new company rebuilt the stone furnaces and enlarged them to 60' x 12'. Additional height was achieved by superimposing upon the stone top an iron cylinder "with bell and hopper." It was hoped that this enlargement of the stacks would materially increase the output. The rebuilt furnaces were put into blast late in 1873 but the anticipated increase in production was not realized, due mainly to the inexperience of the operators. Though rated at 25 tons a day each the furnaces but seldom made more than 10 tons each. They were blown in on a mixture of half charcoal and half coke. Coal was obtained first from the Helena mines and coked in much the same way that wood was converted to charcoal, in shallow pits covered with dust.

A narrow gauge railroad of two and one-half miles was constructed to the ore mines and ten charcoal ovens of 2500 bu. capacity each were built at the furnaces to supplement the outside supply. A total of $200,-000 was spent at this time.

The furnaces were operated for only a few months when the panic of 1873 descended on the iron industry and the plant was shut down.

In 1875 the property was leased by James Thomas and Company which operated the plant for a few months and then gave it up. During this period the future of the iron industry in the Birmingham District seemed very dark; the Irondale Furnace had failed and the Oxmoor plant was idle. At this point a group of citizens, who had invested heavily in Birmingham real estate on the strength of its mineral resources, called a meeting with the object of determining whether Birmingham pig iron could compete successfully in Northern markets. A collection was taken up and sufficient capital was thus raised to make an experimental run of iron using coke as fuel. Only three coal mines were operating in Alabama at this time (at Helena, Warrior and New Castle) and each of them contributed coal. The L & N Railroad contributed free transportation and some cash, and The Eureka Company supplied the No. 2 furnace and the red ore. After some alterations to the stack, the furnace was blown in and on Feb. 28, 1876 the first coke iron was produced at Oxmoor.

This experiment proved a success and the No. 1 furnace was rebuilt to use coke and completed in July 1877. Both the furnaces were now iron shell stacks (No. 1—60' x 16', No. 2—60' x 14') but still had sandstone hearths. With rebuilding of the furnaces, the mines at Helena were increased in capacity and 100 beehive ovens were constructed there. A small battery of Belgian coke ovens was also erected at the furnace to coke Cahaba Coal.

Shortly after the coke iron was made, two groups—one from Louisville and the other from Cincinnati—sought control of the operation. Neither party was successful and for the next few years the plant was operated to the dissatisfaction of everyone. David Sinton of Cincinnati finally gained control in 1886 and operated the property until it was sold on October 18, 1890 to the DeBardeleben Coal and Iron Co. Oxmoor No. 1 had been rebuilt in 1885 and in 1886 the No. 2 furnace was enlarged

Oxmoor Furnaces Nos. 1 and 2 in 1885 before No. 2 Furnace was enlarged to same size as No. 1.

to the same size as the No. 1, 75' x 17'. The combined output of the furnaces was thus increased to about 250 tons a day.

On June 1, 1892 the DeBardeleben Coal and Iron Co. was taken over by the Tennessee Coal, Iron and Railroad Co. and once again the Oxmoor Furnaces changed hands. When the United States Steel Corp. acquired the Tennessee Coal, Iron and Railroad Co. in 1907 the Oxmoor stacks changed managements for the last time.

Under the old Tennessee Coal, Iron & Railroad Co. these furnaces had been rebuilt but not enlarged, the No. 1 in 1902 and the No. 2 in 1899. On October 26, 1907 (the year in which they were acquired by the United States Steel Corp.) the furnaces were blown out and remained idle until February 21, 1913 when they were relighted. Oxmoor continued to operate throughout the World War. After the War, however, it was decided that due to the cost of fuel transportation and the location of the plant, only one stack should operate, the other being used as an alternate.

The last iron to be made at Oxmoor was in May 1927. During 1928 both stacks were dismantled. Thus ended the history of Jefferson County's first blast furnaces—a colorful history of 64 years.

Interior view, Philadelphia Furnace, Florence, showing sand beds in foreground.

PHILADELPHIA FURNACE
Florence, Lauderdale County
1891

THE Florence Land, Mining and Manufacturing Company was incorporated August 31, 1886. Its avowed purpose was "encouragement to all manufacturing." The Florence Land Company, a division of the aforementioned company, donated a tract of 128 acres in the city of Florence on the Tennessee River to the W. B. Wood Furnace Company, which was organized on March 18, 1887, largely by local citizens.

During that year construction of a blast furnace was begun on the donated 128 acres and in its Jan. 14, 1888, issue, the Florence Wave confidently predicted that "the new furnace will be in blast in six months." Shortly after that optimistic notice, however, work was suspended.

On January 11, 1889 the Florence Cotton and Iron Co. was organized with a stated capital of $2,000,000. Three men from Virginia and three from Alabama constituted the incorporators. As an inducement to complete the furnace begun by W. B. Wood Furnace Company, the Florence Land, Mining and Manufacturing Co. contributed to this new company

1000 acres of brown ore lands in Wayne County, Tenn. Work was resumed and the furnace was put into operation early in 1891.

Brown hematite from the Wayne County property was used and coke was brought from Virginia. The furnace, 75' high and 17' in the bosh was rated at 45,000 tons annually. A substantial portion of the output was shipped via the Tennessee River to Northern foundries.

The plant had been in operation for little more than a year when financial difficulties arose. The Florence Cotton and Iron Co. issued $150,000 of 6% bonds on Jan. 1, 1892 to a Philadelphia bank. The depression of 1893 caused the furnace to shut down. The bonds became due and the property was foreclosed. At a public sale Feb. 10, 1897 on the court house steps in Philadelphia, the furnace and lands were bid in for the sum of $25,000.

On June 15, 1899 the property was bought by J. C. Maben of New York City for $107,750. Maben, acting as agent for the Sloss-Sheffield Steel & Iron Co., transferred it to that concern on Nov. 8, 1899.

In 1900 the Sloss Company remodeled the furnace which had been idle since 1892, thereby increasing its annual capacity to 70,000 tons. The remodeled furnace went into blast early in 1901. Brown hematite was supplied from company owned lands in Franklin County as well as from Tennessee. Red ore was brought from Jefferson County to augment the local brown ore supply. Alabama coke from the Sloss mine was used instead of Virginia fuel.

In 1906 the plant was again rebuilt and a modern skip hoist installed. The Philadelphia Furnace, like all of the North Alabama furnaces of that period, was a high cost operation due to the heavy expense of fuel transportation from the Birmingham District. Nevertheless the Philadelphia operated more or less regularly until 1926. In 1928-29 the stack was dismantled.

PIEDMONT FURNACE
Piedmont, Calhoun County
Begun 1890

THE town of Piedmont in Calhoun County is essentially an agricultural community. It is located, however, near large deposits of brown hematite ore. During Alabama's great "Iron Boom" of the late 1880's, a company was formed which planned to industrialize this agricultural community. This company, the Piedmont Land and Improvement Company began erection in 1890 of both a cotton mill and a blast furnace. Foundation of both had been laid when the money ran out. The cotton mill was finally completed by another firm but the furnace was abandoned.

The Piedmont furnace was to have been 60' x 12' and constructed for the use of charcoal. After the stockhouse was completed and the furnace columns placed the project was abandoned in 1891. As late as 1896 it was predicted in the Alabama Geological Survey report that work would be resumed and "completed in 1896." Shortly after that, however, the plant was dismantled and sold for scrap.

The uncompleted Piedmont Furnace is one of the four known plants in the State of Alabama which was either begun or built but which never operated.

ROCK RUN FURNACE
Rock Run, Cherokee County
June 1, 1874

THEODORE and Alfred Royer of Johnstown, Pa., began construction of a small blast furnace in 1873 near Pleasant Gap in Cherokee County, Ala. The original furnace was 38' x 9' with an iron shell and used a vertical elevator to take stock to the top. Cast iron pipe stoves were used to preheat the air. The Rock Run furnace went into blast June 1, 1874. The first ore used was taken from the hill just behind the furnace site; brown ore, however, was found in sufficient quantities within a radius of a few miles to run the plant many years. Charcoal was easily obtained, surrounding forests having been scarcely touched.

The Royer brothers encountered financial difficulties and within less than a year after the furnace was blown in the property was sold on Dec. 6, 1875 by court order to satisfy certain claims. Charles O. Lockard and Thomas S. Ireland purchased the plant for $7,260 and operated the furnace for a short time but without much success. On Aug. 24, 1878 the plant was sold to William Culbertson for $20,000.

John H. Bass, president of the Bass Foundry and Machine Company of Fort Wayne, Indiana purchased the furnace which had been idle since 1875, from Culbertson on Jan. 9, 1880, for $30,000.

Following its purchase, the property was incorporated by the new owners as the Bass Furnace Co. Many improvements were made including the building of a tramway to Pleasant Gap. Prior to the building of this tramway the pig iron was hauled by ox cart the three and one-half miles to the Selma, Rome and Dalton Railroad. In 1881 the furnace was enlarged to 47' x 9' and charcoal kilns were built. A method of roasting the ore was instituted which improved the practice.

At this time most of the iron was shipped to Fort Wayne, Indiana for use by the Bass Company in making car wheels. Later, however, a market for this charcoal iron was found in Pittsburgh for making rolling mill rolls and high quality springs.

In 1894 the name of the operating company was changed to the Bass Foundry and Machine Co. and the furnace was rebuilt to 54.5' x 11.5', the annual capacity being increased to 15,000 G. T. For a time the furnace was known as the Rock Run Iron and Mining Co. but in 1920 the name was changed back to the original, Rock Run Iron Co.

On Christmas Eve, 1928, after 54 years of almost continuous operation, the Rock Run Furnace was blown out. The task of dismantling was begun immediately and completed early in 1929. The company's charter was dissolved on Jan. 12, 1928 and Dr. Gaylord M. Leslie became trustee of the property for the grandchildren of John H. Bass.

Rock Run Furnace, Rock Run. Picture taken 1915.

Round Mountain Furnace about 1880, with cast house on the right and furnace stack enclosed in frame structure on the left.

ROUND MOUNTAIN FURNACE
Cherokee County, near Centre
April 1852

IN 1848 the War with Mexico came to an end with the signing of the Treaty of Guadalupe Hidalgo. During that same year the eldest son of Jacob Stroup, the builder of Cane Creek Furnace, prospected through Cherokee County and purchased several hundred acres of ore lands. This son, Moses, was an iron-master of note in his own right. In Georgia he had erected furnaces and a rolling mill and at the latter had rolled the first railroad strap iron in the South.

The little stone furnace which Moses Stroup began in 1849 was located at the base of Round Mountain, from which it took its name. The plant was situated on the site of a forge owned by William and Henry Milner. Cedar Bluff, the nearest town, was five and one-half miles east of Round Mountain.

On February 11, 1850 Moses Stroup and Wilson Nesbitt incorporated the Alabama Mining and Manufacturing Company. Before the furnace went into blast, Stroup purchased Nesbitt's interest. The following letter was written by Moses Stroup to Michael Tuomey, State Geologist, from Round Mountain Furnace, March 18, 1855, describing operations at the furnace:

"Round Mountain was first put in operation in April, 1852, and has been in operation most of the time since. It has produced two and one-half tons metal per day, and consumed on an average of six hundred fifty bushels of charcoal per day. A portion of the metal is converted into hollow ware and machinery, which is sold in this State, the balance is run into pigs, which find a market in Georgia. The ore used is the red fossiliferous kind. It is taken from the side of the mountain, very near the furnace, where it lies in strata from ten to twenty-four inches in thickness; and is delivered at top of furnace at sixty cents per ton. This ore, when properly treated, makes the best quality of iron for castings and foundry pig.

"The furnace is thirty-two feet high, eight feet in the boshes, and driven by steam power, the steam generated by the waste heat of the furnace, blown by a cold blast. The number of hands employed for all purposes connected with the furnace is forty-five. It is over half a mile from the Coosa River, on which is shipped the pig iron to Rome, Georgia. There is an abundance of good limestone within a mile of the furnace."

Sometime during the year 1855 Stroup sold his holdings to Samuel P. S. Marshall of Eddysville, Ky. John Peter Lesley in his Manufacturer's Guide published in 1859 lists Round Mountain furnace as hot blast and adds that for the three years previous to 1857 the output averaged 11 tons per week. Marshall operated the plant for several years then sold his interest to J. M. Elliott, a steam boat owner of Rome, Georgia.

Shortly after outbreak of the Civil War, the Round Mountain Furnace was leased by Daughdrill and Creigher. In the Spring of 1863 a contract was signed with the Nitre and Mining Bureau and a money advance was obtained from the Confederate Government for the purpose of enlarging the plant.

The following notice appeared in the Montgomery Weekly Mail of May 13, 1863, and indicates the progress of this work:

"Judge Marshall, of Centre, Alabama, one of the operators of the Round Mountain Iron Works, informs the Atlanta Confederacy that the Company have now a large number of hands rebuilding the works, which will probably be completed and ready for operations in two months."

View of dismantled Round Mountain Furnace, showing cylindrical iron top.

A report dated Feb. 14, 1865 from John C. Breckinridge, Secretary of War, to President Jefferson Davis, giving the status of the iron industry in the Confederacy for 1864, states that the Round Mountain Iron Works operated two blast furnaces. There is no other evidence that a second stack was ever operated here. It is possible that Daughdrill and Creigher, lessees of the Round Mountain furnace, may have operated another of the neighboring furnaces but evidence for that assumption is also lacking.

During the war almost all the iron made at Round Mountain Furnace was shipped via the Coosa River to the arsenal at Rome, Georgia and there converted into Confederate ordnance.

The plant was partially destroyed by Gen. Blair late in the Summer of 1864 on the same raid that saw the destruction of Cornwall.

After the war, the furnace remained idle until 1871 when Elliott organized the Round Mountain Coal and Iron Co. The furnace was "rebuilt and put in blast June 1874 after a long rest." The stack was enlarged to 45' x 8-2/3' and the capacity increased to 5,000 tons annually. In 1888 the Elliott Pig Iron Co. was formed and the furnace remodeled, an iron top being installed. Its dimensions were increased to 45' x 9½' and the annual output rated at 6,500 G. T. The Elliott Car Works at

Gadsden, Alabama, under the same family, took almost all the pig iron for use in their car wheels. A portion of the iron, however, was shipped as far as Pittsburgh to be used in the manufacture of rolls for rolling mills.

In 1896 the plant was leased from Elliott by the Round Mountain Furnace Company of Chattanooga, Tenn. By this time charcoal iron had become so expensive by comparison with coke iron that the plant operated only intermittently. It was eventually acquired in 1902 by the Round Mountain Iron & Wood Alcohol Company, the iron becoming almost a by-product of the alcohol distillation process. This company operated the furnace at irregular intervals until it was permanently blown out in December of 1906.

Round Mountain was the first furnace in Alabama to make use of the red fossiliferous ore of the vast Clinton formation. This plant was always a high cost operation due chiefly to the amount of charcoal necessary to reduce the fossiliferous ore. Only the excellence of the iron made the venture practical.

SHELBY FURNACES
Shelby, Shelby County
No. 1—Spring of 1849
No. 2—March of 1863

G OLD was discovered in California in 1848 and by 1849 one of the greatest migrations in civilization was under way.

During that period of national expansion Horace Ware built a small stone furnace in Shelby County. The stack was but 29′ high and 8′ across the bosh. As was the universal practice of that era, the furnace was built against a hillside and the stock brought across a wooden trestle to the top platform. In 1848-49 the forests were still in a virtually uncut condition. It was the rule, therefore, that the furnace be located in close proximity to the ore. At Shelby the ore was within a few hundred yards of the stack and hauled to the stock yard with teams and oxen. This ore (brown hematite) was then roasted before being charged into the furnace.

The land on which the furnace was built had been purchased in 1841 by Horace Ware but a lack of sufficient capital caused a delay in the building of the plant until John M. McClanahan went into partnership with Ware. Some confusion exists as to the date on which the Shelby furnace was put into blast. The following article bearing on this point appeared in the Mobile Herald and was reprinted June 1, 1849 by the State Guard, Wetumpka, Alabama:

> "The Mobile Herald of the 25th of May says, 'We noticed some time since the erection of new Iron works in Shelby County. They are now in full operation. The establishment is in the neighborhood of Columbiana, within 7 miles of the Coosa River, and owned by McClanahan and Ware. The works are operated by steam, and were started about the 1st of March last. Since that time the yield has been 10,000 pounds of pig iron per day, a large portion of which has been sent to the Montgomery foundry where it is pronounced equal in quality to the best Scotch pig iron. The proprietors intend, as soon as navigation ceases, to commence casting hollow ware. We are not advised of the extent of these works, but learn that the expenses of the establishment are $40 per day. The mines from which the ore is obtained are extensive and easily worked.' "

From this and other evidence it is safe to place the date of blowing in at some time early in the year 1849. The census report of 1850 records that Ware and McClanahan owned jointly six slaves, the tax on these slaves amounting to thirty cents. Sometime before 1856 Ware bought out the interest of John M. McClanahan and became the sole owner of the property.

Shelby Furnace No. 2 shortly before being dismantled in 1930.

The lack of transportation facilities greatly hampered the disposal of the product and the operation of the plant. The following letter to Governor Collier, dated May 20, 1850, emphasizes that condition:

> "Columbiana, Shelby County, Ala.
> Our blast furnace is in successful operation and had we facilities for getting to market it would be a fine property.
> (Sgd.) J. M. McClanahan."

As a result of this difficulty, a rather large portion of the output was cast at the furnace into hollow ware and other domestic appliances. A portion, however, was boated down the Coosa River to Montgomery and points further south. Daniel Pratt, the owner of the largest gin manufacturing plant in the South, used Shelby iron almost exclusively.

With slave labor and the proximity of the raw materials, the cost of iron was relatively cheap. An early cost sheet lists:

Ore	$ 2.00
Charcoal	10.00
Limestone	.75
Labor	3.00
Repairs, etc.	1.00
	$16.75

Cost of shipping the iron by river was $6.72 a ton, making a total delivered cost of $23.47 plus drayage to the boats. For the first three years (1849-51) the selling price averaged $30 a ton. In 1852, however, Ware contracted to sell 1,000 tons at $36. For the next four or five years the price varied from $30 to $38. However, during this early period much of the pig iron made by this and other Southern furnaces was bartered for use by little plantation smithies, which required from 50 to 500 pounds of bar iron annually. The following advertisement which appeared in several papers of that era illustrates this practice:

> "SHELBY
> Manufacturing Company
> The Undersigned is now manufacturing a general assortment of
> BAR IRON AND CASTINGS,
> which he offers for sale at the following prices: Bar Iron at wholesale at 4 to 5c, at retail 6 to 7c. Castings from 2½ to 5c per lb. The Bar Iron is superior in point of quality and finish to Swedes, and equal to the celebrated Norway Iron, which costs $140 per ton in New York. County produce taken, as also waste or scrap iron— wrought at $30 and cast at $20 per ton at this depot. TERMS— CASH.
> Horace Ware."

The first hot blast equipment in Alabama was installed by Ware at Shelby in 1855 when he rebuilt the plant. In a letter dated July 5, 1854 to Wm. P. Browne, Ware observes, "We are in a great hurry to complete our hot blast castings to get our furnace in operation as early as possible."

On Feb. 4, 1858, the property was incorporated as the Shelby County Iron Manufacturing Co., comprising "the 5,000 acres now held by Horace Ware, on which is the iron furnace." A further provision of the act of incorporation forbade "the sale of spirituous liquors within three miles of said furnace." In that same year (1858) Ware began the building of his rolling mill, which, however, did not go into production until April 11, 1860. And in that year 1858 the wooden charcoal sheds, cast house and stock trestle burned.

The Bulletin of the American Iron Association, published in 1858, presented some little known facts about the Shelby Furnace:

"The proprietor writes again that the blast of 1855 was so small (230 tons in 14 weeks run) because an experimental hot blast proved, 'a most signal failure,' and encloses the following statement of his founder, Mr. Babington, which of course he endorses. 'I have been blowing and managing furnaces for the past twenty-five years in Pennsylvania, Kentucky, Ohio, Tennessee, Maryland, etc., and have never before found ore that would yield fifty per cent regularly in a furnace. A good furnace here will make 8 to 10 tons per day as easy as ore in those States would 6 to 8 tons with the same amount of coal. Estimate of cost of one ton of pig metal; cost to raise one ton of ore 37½ cts.; hauling 25; burning 25, cleaning ready for use 50—$1.37½; 2 tons of ore to one ton of pig—$2.75, charcoal 113 bushels at 4 cents—$4.52, Founders' wages 1.00, hands' wages 1.25,—$9.52, the furnace running 4 tons per day; if 6 to 8 tons, the cost would be reduced 10 percent. Add 48 cents for oil, smiths, carpenters, etc. which would be abundance, and we have the cost of a ton of pig metal in Alabama $10.00. In Pennsylvania in my time it was $15 to $16; in Kentucky it cost about the same; in Ohio $12 to $14; in Maryland $17 to $18; in Tennessee we always count on $15. I have made calculations at different furnaces. I have run this (Shelby) furnace seven months under unfavorable circumstances and have not used over 115 bushels of coal to the ton of pig iron. The hard Round Mountain ore requires 250 to 300 bushels.'"

In this same publication is the following:

"SHELBY Furnace.—7 miles west of Coosa River, 17 miles E. of Montevallo, 62 miles N. of Montgomery, 55 m. N. of Wetumpka, on the line of one of the contemplated routes for the Alabama Central R. R. Has two wooden cylinders 3½ diam. x 3½ stroke, 8 revolutions. Ore, fibrous brown hematite, from a ridge 1 mile long by ½ mile wide, extending northwestwardly from furnace; present opening 300 yards N. of furnace; old opening half mile north. The whole surface of ridge is covered with ore averaging 50 per cent. (Specimens may be seen at office of Association) Sends metal to Selma, Montgomery, Mobile, New Orleans and Columbus, Ga. The furnace has averaged from 25 May to 25 September 1857, 4½ to 5 tons per day. In 1854 made (hot) 68,282 lbs. pig No. 1; 6,000 lbs. scrap; 19,500 lbs. forge pig No. 1; 1,300 lbs. No. 2; 3,000 lbs. scrap; 4,895 lbs. of machinery and hollow ware; (cold) 124,310 lbs. pig No. 1, 105,100 lbs. No. 2, 132,900 scrap, 846 forge scrap. In 1855 tried to put in a hot blast without success. In 1856 made 965¼ tons foundry iron.

In another part of this publication appeared the following:

"For sale: Furnace with $5,000 worth of equipage and 6,000 acres of arable timber land, including the above ore ridge and another good one with beds of limestone (the ore now used is 3½ m. N. E.) and water power (3½ m. S. E. of the furnace). Camp Branch and Valley Forges, and 170 acres; and 140 acres of coal land near the latter, and the Alabama Coal Co.'s R. R.—for $80,000 cash (or $10,000 cash and 90,000 in six annual payments; or $10,000 and an agreement to put up a rolling mill for $25,000, run it 5 years and pay the difference between the iron made and the ordinary English and American iron) or otherwise. Mr. Ware would agree to make a 5 mile road to the Columbiana Station, to haul 2 tons a day the horse, for $600. Bituminous coal can be delivered at the furnace at $1.25 per ton. Charcoal costs 3 c. a bushel. The works are at the southern extremity of the coal field. An unlimited market for bar iron exists. The present price is 7-8 c. per lb. The country is a summer resort."

During the eighteen months which followed outbreak of the Civil War the cost of slave hire advanced from $175.00 a year to $250.00 and $300.00 and the cost of supplies 30 to 50%. On March 18, 1862, Ware sold a 6/7 interest in the property for the sum of $150,000. Purchasers were John W. and James W. Lapsley, Henry H. Ware, John R. Kenan, John M. McClanahan and A. T. Jones. Jones, though but 33 years old, was elected president. In 1863 one of the incorporators, J. W. Lapsley, was captured by the Union Army in Kentucky while looking for puddlers.

On Nov. 20, 1862 this new company had the name of the organization changed to the Shelby Iron Company. Shortly after the sale in 1862

We use in our blast furnaces a patent filler & thimble which we think is of much service. It acts to throw the ore and flux to the inner walls of the furnace & then by its own gravity it draws to the centre of the furnace. In the ordinary way of charging the ore is thrown into the middle of the furnace & descends straight down without being properly mixed with the coal. I an- nex a sketch of this apparatus.

a - is the inside of the stack which runs up from a 9 ft bosh straight to a 48 to 52 in. Trunnel head.

b. is a thimble of wrought iron 4 ft long and of the diameter to fill the trun- nle head. = c is an opening through the stack, at the bottom of the thimble through which the gas is taken under the boilers.

d. is the ore filler with movable conical bottom. When it is run over the trunnel head, the bottom is lowered by means of the lever and the ore is thrown to the inner wall.

Original sketch and description of first bell and hopper installation in Alabama (about 1863) on Shelby Furnace No. 1 at Shelby.

the new owners signed a contract (of a more or less mandatory nature) with the Confederate government which stipulated a certain tonnage of pig and bar iron per quarter. The control by the government, of the Shelby company was so rigid that it was forbidden to roll rail for the railroad which the company planned to construct to connect with the Alabama and Tennessee Rivers Railroad at Columbiana. When, in defiance of the order, the company did complete the railroad, the government threatened to assume its management.

A new and larger blast furnace was begun in 1862 at Shelby and put into blast during March of 1863. This new stack was constructed of brick, made by slave labor on the site of the plant. Capacity of this new furnace was 15 to 20 tons a day compared with the 8 tons a day of the smaller original stone furnace.

In the Spring of 1864 an experiment was tried substituting raw bituminous coal for charcoal. A letter from the company to the Nitre and Mining Bureau states: "This coal in the raw state was exclusively used as fuel, and produced an iron of so good a quality, that no perceptible difference could be observed." This coal was obtained from one of the company's mines near Montevallo. This was the first such experiment in Alabama but was not made a practice due to the insufficiency of coal at that time.

The Confederate arsenal at Selma used most of the iron produced at Shelby. Part of the armor plate for the famous C. S. S. Tennessee was rolled at Shelby. The quality of the iron may be judged from the fact that the "Tennessee" successfully withstood several broadsides at the Battle of Mobile Bay despite the short range. Undoubtedly Shelby supplied more iron to the Selma arsenal than any other plant in Alabama but the exact tonnage would be difficult to estimate. The Shelby Iron Co. continued to supply this arsenal until April of 1865 when a detachment of Federal raiders under Gen. Wilson destroyed the plant.

After Wilson's raid the Shelby Iron Co. had assets consisting of a ruined plant and a few hundred tons of pig and bar iron; its liabilities were debts contracted for the hire of slaves, and for supplies. Consequently liquidation was necessary. Thus in 1868 the property was acquired by a group of New England capitalists. The new management began the construction of a modern furnace to replace the original stone stack built in 1848. This new stack, 60′ x 14′ went into blast in 1873. It was one of the first iron shell furnaces built after the war.

The brick furnace built in 1863 was dismantled in 1888 and a new furnace duplicating the one built in 1873 was blown in during 1889.

There was little or no market in the South at this time, hence a great portion of the iron was shipped via Savannah, Ga. to New York and Philadelphia for use in car wheels and other castings demanding charcoal pig iron.

During 1890 the Shelby Co. was acquired by New York capital. The plant operated very regularly until about 1903 but the cost of warm blast charcoal pig iron was too great for any save very specialized castings. As a consequence there was not enough demand to justify the operation of both furnaces. In 1906 the Shelby No. 1 was blown in on a coke burden, the first fuel other than charcoal to be used at Shelby since the Civil War experiment with the bituminous coal.

Both furnaces were used during the World War period but after the Armistice only one furnace was operated and that one only part time. The last iron made at the Shelby Iron Co. was produced in August 1923. In June 1929 the historic furnaces were sold to a Birmingham firm for scrap. Work of dismantling the stacks was completed in 1930.

SLOSS CITY FURNACES
Birmingham, Jefferson County

Sloss City Furnaces
No. 1—April 12, 1882
No. 2—Oct. 1883

North Birmingham Furnaces
No. 1—Oct. 1888
No. 2—Feb. 1889

A LICE FURNACE No. 1 in Birmingham had gone into blast Nov. 30, 1880 and was producing a good grade of coke pig iron. Col. H. F. DeBardeleben was not only one of the owners of the Alice but he also supplied all the fuel from his coal mines. Success of the Alice furnace prompted DeBardeleben to suggest to J. W. Sloss the erection of two more blast furnaces in Birmingham. Col. DeBardeleben contracted to furnish all the coal for five years at cost plus 10%. Sloss alone could not finance the project and a large part of the capital was supplied by the Louisville and Nashville Railroad and by B. F. Guthrie. Thus in 1881 the Sloss Furnace Company was formed with Sloss as president and Guthrie as vice-president.

A tract of about 50 acres was purchased on the north edge of Birmingham on what is now First Avenue and on this site a blast furnace was begun in 1881 and blown in on April 12, 1882. This stack was 65' x 16'. In 1882 a second and larger furnace, Sloss No. 2, with a stack 75' x 16½', was begun. Due to a shortage of coke this furnace was not blown in for more than a year after completion.

At this time, all the coke was supplied by the Pratt Coal and Coke Co. J. W. Sloss had purchased two small bodies of ore, one near Steele in St. Clair County, and one on Red Mountain. This supply was inadequate and had to be supplemented by the purchase of ore from independent mining companies.

Despite the fact that the Sloss Company owned but a small portion of its raw material requirements, pig iron was produced here in 1883 for $11.90 a ton which was considered quite low during that era.

In 1886 an option on the Sloss Furnace Company was secured by a group of local men and a new company, the Sloss Iron & Steel Company, was organized on Nov. 29, 1886 with an authorized capital of $3,000,000. Organizers of the new company did not have sufficient capital to exercise their option so the necessary funds had to be raised in Wall Street. This was successfully accomplished and the new man-

View of Sloss City Furnaces, First Avenue in Birmingham, as they looked in 1889.

North Birmingham furnaces of Sloss-Sheffield Steel & Iron Co., just after completion of North Birmingham No. 2 in 1889.

agement assumed control, immediately thereafter instituting a program of expansion. Additional land was acquired in North Birmingham and construction of two new furnaces was started. The Coalburg Coal and Coke Company was also bought and red ore property near Bessemer was purchased.

The North Birmingham Furnaces, know as the Sloss No. 3 and No. 4, were both 75′ x 17′. The No. 3 was blown in during October 1888 and the No. 4 went into blast during February of 1889.

Even before the No. 3 was blown in, however, the new Sloss Iron & Steel Company had become involved in serious financial difficulties. Its new management was in the hands of men wholly unfamiliar with the iron business and they greatly over expanded. In 1888 this management resigned and was succeeded by men of experience. Under their direction the company slowly regained its financial health and in 1899 was reorganized as the Sloss-Sheffield Steel & Iron Company. This new company acquired three North Alabama furnaces—the Lady Ensley, the Hattie Ensley and the Philadelphia Furnace—which had failed and were in the courts. Failure was due principally to the long freight haul on purchased coke, some of which came from Virginia and some from the Birmingham district. Along with the three furnaces, the Sloss-Sheffield Steel & Iron Company also acquired large tracts of brown hematite ore lands in North Alabama and Tennessee. With a company owned source of fuel thus made available, the furnaces were operated economically for many years.

Other coal and ore lands were purchased and in 1900 with the acquisition of these various properties, the new Sloss-Sheffield Steel & Iron Company had absorbed thirteen smaller companies. To supply all seven furnaces the company operated 1,000 beehive coke ovens at five coal mines.

In 1920 a battery of 120 Semet-Solvay by-product coke ovens was built at North Birmingham and a number of the old beehive ovens were abandoned. In 1923 five more blast furnaces were acquired when the Cole Furnaces (only one of the original three was then standing), the Etowah Furnaces and the Clifton Furnaces were taken over. Since the founding of the Sloss Company in 1881 that company has owned a total of twelve blast furnaces in Alabama, a number equaled only by the Tennessee Coal, Iron & Railroad Co.

Due to the high cost of assembling the raw materials, the Sloss-Sheffield Steel & Iron Company has now abandoned and dismantled all its blast furnaces except the four in the Birmingham District.

The four existing furnaces (the City Furnaces and the North Birmingham furnaces) are of the following dimensions and capacities:

	Height	Hearth	Bosh	Annual Capacity
No. 1	83′ 8″	15′ 0″	21′ 0″	148900
No. 2	81′ 2″	15′ 4″	20′ 3″	141200
No. 3	80′ 10″	12′ 8″	17′ 10″	118050
No. 4	80′ 10″	12′ 2″	17′ 11″	118050
				526200 G. T.

The Sloss-Sheffield Steel & Iron Co. is one of the three remaining merchant pig iron producers now operating in the South.

STONEWALL FURNACE

(Known also as Langdon Furnace)
Cherokee County, near Rock Run
1873

H. D. COTHRAN of Rome, Georgia organized the Stonewall Iron Co. in 1872 and began erection of a small blast furnace on the main line of the Selma, Rome and Dalton Railroad about three miles from the Georgia state line in the County of Cherokee. This furnace was one of the first iron shell stacks in the state, 40' high and 11' in the bosh, with a daily capacity of 15 tons.

Brown hematite ore was obtained within a few miles of the plant in both Alabama and Georgia and hauled to the furnace in wagons. The charcoal was supplied from the surrounding forests.

Stonewall furnace was blown in during 1873 but due to the severe panic of that year, the plant was shut down after operating for only a short time. Late in 1875 the property was acquired by J. W. Bones who put the furnace into blast early in 1876. The furnace did not operate regularly but only during periods of high pig iron prices.

In 1879 W. H. Harrison leased the furnace. A closed top was installed but the furnace was not otherwise altered. Coke instead of charcoal was used as fuel. At that time Alabama was producing scarcely enough coke to supply the other four coke furnaces of the state, hence it is probable that the coke supply for Stonewall was obtained from sources outside the state. Within less than a year, however, operations were suspended. It is interesting to note that this East Alabama furnace was one of the very first users of coke in the state despite its location far from a coal field.

In 1882 the property was leased again and another attempt was made to operate, this time using charcoal. Once again the furnace was blown out after a short run.

The Stonewall Furnace was idle from 1882 until 1890. In 1885 the plant was classified as "abandoned." In 1889, however, the Langdon Iron Co. was formed and the furnace was entirely rebuilt. The stack was enlarged to 46' x 11½' and the capacity doubled to 13,500 tons annually. The new stack went into blast in May 1890 making "warm blast charcoal car wheel iron."

A blowing engine of the "walking beam" type was employed. This engine was very similar in design to those in use on river steamers of that day. The piston had a very long stroke and worked in a large wooden cylinder, lubricated with a form of home-made lye soap, which, due to the heat of friction, crystalized into a substance resembling glass.

The Stonewall plant was shut down in the Spring of 1893 and was never operated again. In 1894 the Alabama Ore and Railroad Co. acquired the property and mined some ore but did not attempt to run the furnace. Eventually, in 1896, the National Bank of Augusta took over the property and offered it for sale. Some time between 1899 and 1901 the plant was dismantled.

During the 27 years of the furnace's existence, it did not operate for more than four or five years. The Stonewall, like a number of other furnaces, must be classified as a fair weather operation.

View taken in 1925 of Talladega Furnace in Talladega.

TALLADEGA FURNACE
Talladega, Talladega County
Oct. 5, 1889

THE Talladega Iron & Steel Co., Ltd., was organized in 1888 by a group of English capitalists. Some mineral lands within a few miles of Talladega were purchased. On the outskirts of this town a furnace was built on the site where General Andrew Jackson, on November 9, 1813 defeated the Cherokee Indians in the last battle in Alabama to establish the supremacy of the white man. On Oct. 5, 1889 the furnace went into blast, using coke shipped in from Virginia. After 1899 coal was obtained from company owned lands in St. Clair county and coked at the furnace. Brown hematite ore was mined from the company lands within a few miles of Talladega.

The Talladega furnace was 72' x 18' and averaged about 750 tons a week. The plant was never an economical unit for several reasons. Even before construction of the furnace was begun, the company's management had controversy with the East Tennessee, Virginia and Georgia Railroad concerning freight rates, as a result of which, the plant was located on the narrow gauge line of the Birmingham and Atlanta Railroad, thus necessitating the rehandling of all materials both for construction and operation. The long fuel haul as well as the uncertainty of the ore supply also approved a severe handicap.

After a run of little more than two years, the Talladega furnace was blown out due to these difficulties and the low selling price of pig iron. In 1892 the English company went into the hands of a receiver. In 1893 the Talladega Furnace Co. was organized and took over the property in 1894. The furnace was blown in the following year but operated for only a few months. In 1896 the plant was purchased by the Alabama Iron & Railway Co. which put the furnace into blast early in 1897. Once again the Talladega furnace proved too high cost an operation and after a run of less than a year was again blown out.

In June 1899 the Northern Alabama Coal, Iron & Railroad Co. acquired the property under a foreclosure sale. This company rebuilt the furnace, increasing the height to 75', and constructed at the furnace a battery of 122 beehive coke ovens, and at Wattsville, the coal mine, another battery of 60 ovens. The rebuilt furnace went into blast in the middle of 1900 and continued in blast until October 1903 when the low price of pig iron forced a shut down.

Once again the plant remained idle for a long period. During the World War, a company was formed to rebuild the plant. This group lacked the money to put the furnace into blast and the property was then taken over by a subsidiary of the Japanese Mitsui Co. A total of approximately $220,000 was spent by the Japanese to put the Talladega furnace into blast. About 2,000 tons were made here before the Armistice, 1,000 tons of which were on the high seas at the time. This iron was shipped through the Port of Pensacola.

The Talladega furnace was blown out shortly after the Armistice and never was operated again. In 1930 the stack and all accessories were dismantled for scrap. The Talladega Furnace Properties, Inc. were the owners under Alexander Tison, Trustee. It is claimed that the first Bessemer (low phosphorus) pig iron produced in Alabama and shipped North was made at the Talladega furnace in 1890.

TANNEHILL FURNACES

(Known also as Roup's Valley Iron Works, Sanders Furnaces)
Tuscaloosa County, near Bucksville
No. 1—1859—1861
No. 2 & No. 3—1863

HISTORY of the Tannehill Furnaces, remains of which are located in Tuscaloosa County about two miles southeast of the present settlement at Bucksville, has been the object of much speculation, true in part but mostly fiction.

The land on which these furnaces were built was granted to Abner McGehee by the United States in 1829. McGehee engaged Daniel Hillman to erect a forge and operate it. The forge was operated irregularly until the property was sold in 1840 to Ninion (or Ninian) Tannehill and J. B. Green; four years later Green sold his interest to Tannehill.

It is believed by some that the iron-master, Moses Stroup, built a blast furnace here in 1855, although there is absolutely no record to authenticate such a claim. A son-in-law of Stroup, John Alexander, bought the Tannehill property in 1857. J. P. Lesley in the Bulletin of the American Iron Association of 1858 lists "Stroup's Forge." An exact description of the land is given (Township 20, Range 5 W, Section 33) and states:

> "Bloomery, making bars for home market from hematite ores, brown and fiberous, from neighborhood. Made in 1857, up to Oct. 1, 60,394 lbs. in 110 days."

Despite the fact that Moses Stroup is listed as the owner, the land records indicate that the furnace site never actually belonged to Stroup. Had there been a furnace at that point in 1858, Lesley would most certainly have given a description of it.

It is most probable that a small stone blast furnace was begun near the site of the forge sometime between 1859 and 1861. And there is no doubt that Moses Stroup superintended the construction of the stack but that John Alexander was the owner. Stone for this furnace was quarried locally by slave labor and hauled by oxen team to the furnace site. When the stone stack was completed, a wooden trestle was built connecting the furnace top to the adjoining bank for the purpose of charging the furnace. The little stack was 30′ high and 8½′ in the bosh and produced not over five or six tons a day.

Tannehill (Single) Furnace No. 1. Hillside on left was used for filling furnace.

View of the three Tannehill Furnaces. Single furnace on left, double furnace on right.

It is thought by many that the furnace was lined with brick from Stowbridge, England. When the difficulties of transportation of that age are considered, this seems most improbable. More likely the brick was made by slaves from local clay.

Location of the furnace was in a bend of Roup's Creek. A wooden flume furnished the water to an overshot wheel, which was mounted on a wooden axle that turned in stone bearings. To one end of this axle was attached a cam which operated the huge blowing bellows by means of a lever. The stream also furnished the power to operate the forge hammer.

The little furnace made the usual line of domestic and agricultural implements which were disposed of around the countryside. No doubt as much was bartered as was sold; country produce was as necessary to the operation as money because the slaves, hired from their owners, had to be both fed and clothed.

Slaves dug the brown hematite ore from open pits on the Goethite deposit and hauled it the two miles to the furnace bank. Later a little tramway, the remains of which can still be seen, was built for this purpose. Wood was cut from the pine forests and burned in dust pits. Pig iron cost $17.40 a ton here the year prior to the Civil War.

In 1862 John Alexander sold the furnace to Wm. L. Sanders. Stroup remained as superintendent for a few months, then accepted a position with the Red Mountain Iron & Coal Co.

On March 23, 1863, Sanders signed a contract with the Nitre and Mining Bureau, an existing copy of which notes that Sanders *"agrees to manufacture and deliver on the cars of the Alabama and Tennessee River Railroad, at Montevallo, 4,000 tons of pig iron per annum."* From the furnaces to Montevallo was a distance of 18 miles over which the iron was hauled by oxen. In the contract it was further agreed that any amount of pig iron produced in excess of the 4,000 tons belonged to the Government. From available information it is safe to say that Sanders never delivered a fraction of the iron stipulated in the contract, which contained this provision:

"To enable the party of the first part (W. L. Sanders) to finish the furnace now under construction, it is agreed that the Government shall advance $50,000 in bonds of the Confederate States of America."

A price schedule for the year 1864 was appended which stipulated No. 1 Cold Blast pig iron at $160 a ton. Sanders used the advance to build a double furnace and put in a steam plant to take the place of the crude and unreliable water power. His new furnaces were almost a duplicate of the older stack.

Those iron works, under contract to the Confederate States, were supplied with skilled labor from the army. The following note illustrates this point:

"Roup's Valley Iron Works—June 14, 1864
Shelby Iron Co.
   Gentlemen:
     Gleason, an Irishman by birth, by trade a blacksmith, age about 40 years and being attached to me has deserted. If he should apply at your Works for employment, please refuse him and inform me.
     Very respectfully,
              Wm. L. Sanders."

Gen. Wilson of the Union Army concentrated his forces at Elyton in Jefferson County. His objective was the arsenal at Selma. He divided his command, sending part under Gen. Croxton toward Tuscaloosa and the remainder under himself to the Southeast.

Sometime early in April of 1865 a detachment of Croxton's brigade on its march toward Tuscaloosa came upon and burned Roup's Valley Iron Works. Late in that same year John Alexander bought the property back from Sanders. He may have planned to rebuild the plant but failed to do so and in 1868 he sold it to David Thomas. In that manner the Republic Steel Corporation eventually obtained the property and is now the owner.

TECUMSEH FURNACE
Cherokee County, near Rock Run
Feb. 19, 1874

WITH General Willard Warner of the Union Army as its president and manager, the Tecumseh Iron Company was formed in 1873 with a capital of $100,000 supplied by residents of Maine, New York, Massachusetts, Illinois and Ohio. With this capital a furnace was built on the Selma, Rome and Dalton Railroad in Cherokee County, only a few miles from the Stonewall and Rock Run furnaces in Alabama and the Aetna furnace in Georgia, all of which were constructed about the same time. The plant was named in honor of William Tecumseh Sherman, the Federal general, who made the long remembered "march to the sea" through Georgia during the Civil War. In later years, General Sherman visited his friend, General Warner, several times at Tecumseh.

At the time the Tecumseh furnace was blown in on February 19, 1874, it was considered one of the most pretentious in the South. The stack, entirely of iron, was 60' x 12', "with open top soon to be closed by bell and hopper." The furnace was rated at 25 tons per day but due mainly to faulty design did not produce over 15 tons.

When the furnace was first blown in it had an open top and a sandstone hearth but it was blown out on April 4, 1874 to put in a closed top and "a fire brick hearth with water jackets," then blown in again on June 19, 1875. Improvements made in the furnace increased its output to about 25 tons a day of "foundry, mill and chilling irons."

From June 1875, "the furnace ran 7 years, 1 month and 18 days on one hearth without blowing out"—a rather remarkable record of a continuous operation.

Most of the brown ore used in Tecumseh Furnace was mined within a few hundred yeards of the furnace, though some was obtained from Polk County, Georgia on the state line. Beehive charcoal ovens at the plant supplied the fuel.

Tecumseh Furnace operated almost constantly until about 1886, at which time charcoal became harder to obtain and more expensive. Cost of charcoal iron consequently increased and demand for it declined because of the high price.

From 1886 until October 1890 Tecumseh Furnace operated only at intervals. On the latter date it was blown out and never relighted. However, the Baker Hill brown ore deposit, within a short distance of the furnace, continued to be mined for some years thereafter. In order to acquire this source of ore the Birmingham Coal & Iron Company purchased the entire property of the Tecumseh Iron Company (about 10,000 acres) on January 14, 1909. The ore mined on Baker Hill was thereafter shipped to the Vanderbilt furnaces in Birmingham.

On April 4, 1912 the Woodward Iron Company bought the Birmingham Coal & Iron Company and thus acquired the Tecumseh property. Just prior to the World War, the old furnace, after being idle for more than twenty years, was dismantled for scrap.

THOMAS FURNACES

Jefferson County, near Birmingham
No. 1—May 15, 1888
No. 2—Feb. 22, 1890
No. 3—June 13, 1902

SHORTLY after the Civil War, Giles Edwards, "iron-maker" at the Shelby furnace during the war, advised his friend, David Thomas of Pennsylvania, to purchase ore and coal lands in Alabama. The Thomas family were iron-masters of Pennsylvania who had been connected with the iron business for several generations. Edwards was familiar with the location and extent of much of the lands and Thomas delegated him to make certain purchases, among which were the Tannehill site and the brown ore deposit at Goethite, a few miles distant.

On Dec. 30, 1868, the Pioneer Mining and Manufacturing Co. was formed as a land holding company with a capital of $500,000. Among its organizers were David and John Thomas and Giles Edwards. Baylis Grace, an early settler at "Grace's Gap", acted as Thomas' agent in the acquisition of additional ore property in Jefferson County. Twenty years later the Hawkins cotton plantation was purchased by the Pioneer Company and the town of Thomas laid out some four miles southwest of Birmingham.

During the great Alabama "Iron Boom" of the 1880's, Mr. Thomas began the erection at Thomas of his first furnace, which was put into blast May 15, 1888. Edwin Thomas, grandson of the founder, was placed in charge of the operation. The first stack was 75' x 17' and used eight 5" tuyeres. The original burden was figured to be 1/2 to 2/3 red ore and 1/2 to 1/3 brown ore from the Tannehill section. At the outset the Pioneer Company was unable to mine and coke sufficient fuel and the Cahaba Coal Company supplied it until a battery of 150 beehive ovens could be built at the plant to coke the company coal, mined at Sayreton.

The Pioneer Company blew in a second duplicate furnace Feb. 22, 1890. A feature of these two furnaces is the long inclined skip bridge from stock house to furnace top.

In 1898 an option was secured on the Pioneer capital stock and in 1899 was exercised by the Republic Iron & Steel Co. A new furnace, the Thomas No. 3, blown in on June 13, 1902, was the largest in the Birmingham district at that time. Capacity of this furnace was rated at 250 tons per day. There was much speculation as to whether a furnace of such size could be operated on Alabama red hematite. In 1903 the No. 2

View of Thomas Furnace No. 2, taken 1890, showing long skip incline and furnace bonnet.

was enlarged to 90′ x 18′, the same size as the new No. 3. The No. 1 was likewise rebuilt to 85′ x 20′.

Since 1903 the furnaces have been remodeled several times. In 1939 the smallest stack, the No. 3, was dismantled. Both the No. 1 and No. 2 now have 16′ hearths, furnace No. 1 being 83′-4½″ high and No. 2, 88′-6″ measured from iron notch to top platform.

On Oct. 21, 1925 a battery of 57 Koppers-Becker by-product coke ovens with a daily capacity of 1200 tons was put in operation at the furnaces.

In April 1930 all the properties of the Republic Iron & Steel Co. were taken over by the Republic Steel Corporation. Since 1937 the Thomas Furnaces have been supplying iron to the Republic Steel Corporation's steel plant at Alabama City.

TRUSSVILLE FURNACE
Trussville, Jefferson County
April 1889

A GROUP of men from Uniontown, Pa., incorporated the Birmingham Furnace & Manufacturing Co. on Dec. 21, 1886 with an authorized capital of $1,500,000. In 1887 they purchased from the Trussville and Cahaba River Land Co. a tract of land near the town of Trussville and about 15 miles northeast of Birmingham.

Building of a furnace was begun on this tract in 1887, a large portion of the material being supplied from the dismantled Lemont Furnace in Fayette County, Pa. The completed stack, 65' high and 17½' in the bosh, was blown in during April 1889. From that date until the middle of 1893, the furnace was in blast, but due to the diminishing demand for pig iron during this period it was then blown out. In 1894 a trustee was named for the bondholders and the company was reorganized as the Trussville Furnace Co. The stack was remodeled (65' x 16½') and put into blast late in 1896 but operated for only a few months before being again blown out.

Chief difficulty at the Trussville Furnace was the high cost of raw material transportation. Red hematite was mined within a few miles of the furnace but not in sufficient quantity to supply the entire demand so that additional ore had to be purchased from the Birmingham and Bessemer Districts to supplement the local supply. Brown hematite was brought from as far away as Georgia, and coke from Birmingham.

On September 1, 1899 the Trussville Furnace, Mining and Manufacturing Co. was organized by a group of local men to take over the Trussville Furnace property. The furnace was blown in sometime in 1901 but again operated for only a few months.

On July 10, 1902 the property was sold to the Lacey-Buek Iron Co., a Tennessee corporation. This company began rebuilding of the furnace and construction of beehive coke ovens. The stack was enlarged from 65' to 80' and the bosh was widened by 6". More important, however, as an independent source of raw materials, was the Crudup ore mine in Etowah County and the Graves Coal Mine in Jefferson County which belonged to the Lacey-Buek Company. The rebuilt furnace was rated at 70,000 tons annually. When blown in during 1903 it was christened the "Ella."

Under the Lacey-Buek Company the plant continued in operation until it was acquired on July 1, 1906 by the Southern Steel Company when it was rebuilt but not enlarged. The Southern Steel Company bankrupted in 1907 and in 1909 the Southern Iron & Steel Co. took over control. In 1911 this company defaulted on its bonds and the Trussville Furnace property passed to the Michigan Trust Co. The furnace had been blown out the year previous in 1910.

The Trussville furnace remained idle from 1910 until 1918. In 1917 Chicago interests acquired the property from the Michigan Trust Co. and in that same year the Birmingham-Trussville Iron Co. was organized. The furnace plant and the beehive ovens were repaired as rapidly as possible to take advantage of the World War prices. The furnace was blown in during the Spring of 1918 and operated until the Spring of 1919. In 1933 the Trussville Furnace was dismantled and the land on which it stood was sold in 1935 to the Birmingham Homestead, Inc., a Federal Housing Administration project.

Vanderbilt Furnaces, about 1926.

VANDERBILT FURNACES
North Birmingham, Jefferson County
No. 1—Aug. 23, 1890
No. 2—May 8, 1908

THE Vanderbilt Steel & Iron Co. was organized in 1889 with New York and Tennessee capital. On Feb. 9, 1890 ground was broken in North Birmingham (near Boyles) for the erection of a blast furnace. Within a little less than seven months, on Aug. 23, 1890, the plant was blown in. Many furnaces of that period were given feminine names and the Vanderbilt Furnace, in accordance with the custom, was christened "Clara." Its dimensions were 65' x 14' and its rating 22,500 tons a year of "a strong low phosphorus foundry pig iron."

The Vanderbilt company had to depend largely on other concerns for its supply of both ore and coke. As a consequence of this condition operation of the plant proved uneconomical and less than six months after being blown in the company was in the hands of a trustee. The furnace was blown out in 1892 and continued idle until 1899.

On Aug. 12, 1896 the plant was acquired by local interests, who sold it a year later (Oct. 4, 1897) to the Spathite Iron Co. This company had

also purchased the North Alabama furnace at Florence which was producing so-called "Spathite pig iron." This product enjoyed a price advantage of $1.00 a ton but the high cost of ore transportation (from Iron
City, Tenn.) caused the project to be abandoned.

E. M. Tutwiler, President and founder of the Tutwiler Coal, Coke
and Iron Co. acquired the plant on March 28, 1899. The Tutwiler Company had large holdings on the Pratt seam and an ore mine (Songo) on
Red Mountain and for the first time the furnace thus had available a re-
liable supply of ore and coal. The Vanderbilt furnace was completely
remodeled in 1899, enlarged to 76½' x 15½' and the capacity increased
to 54,000 tons.

On May 23, 1906 the Tutwiler Coal, Coke & Iron Co. sold out its
interests to the Birmingham Iron Co., which merged with the Birmingham
Coal Co. in 1907 to form the Birmingham Coal and Iron Co. Construction of a second furnace was begun by this company and on May 8, 1908
it was put into blast. This second furnace, the Vanderbilt No. 2, was 80' x
18' and had an annual capacity of 85,000 tons. A battery of beehive
ovens was built at Vanderbilt to coke coal from the Mulga Mine; another
battery of ovens was built at the Short Creek mine. In 1909 the
Tecumseh Iron Co. was bought and the brown ore from that property
was used at Vanderbilt.

The Woodward Iron Co. purchased the Birmingham Coal and Iron
Co. on April 4, 1912. In that transaction a check was written for $1,000,-
000 as a part payment and for some time that stood as the largest private
check ever written in the State of Alabama.

The two Vanderbilt furnaces were operated more or less regularly
by the Woodward Iron Co. until 1929 when they were blown out. Transportation of raw materials to the plant made the operation uneconomical
and in 1935 the furnaces were dismantled and sold for scrap.

One of these furnaces was crated and boxed after dismantling for
shipment overseas, having been sold by the salvage contractor to an iron
company in China. While awaiting arrival of a ship at Mobile, Alabama,
fire damaged this material while it was stored on the State Docks.

Williamson Furnace, which stood just south of First Avenue and Fourteenth Street, Birmingham, about 1890.

WILLIAMSON FURNACE

Birmingham, Jefferson County

Oct. 1886

BETWEEN 1880 and 1886 no less than six blast furnaces were built along First Avenue in Birmingham, Jefferson County, Alabama. The last of these, the Williamson, was erected just south of First Avenue at Fourteenth Street.

Charles P. Williamson and James B. Simpson incorporated the Williamson Iron Co. on June 13, 1885 with a capitalization of $150,000, of which $20,000 was subscribed by the Elyton Land Co. This subscription was paid on July 1, 1885 by a deed to the land on which the new furnace was to be located.

The Williamson Furnace was blown in during Oct. of 1886. The stack was 65' high and 12-2/3' in the bosh. Capacity of the plant was 1250 tons a month of "foundry and forge pig iron." The Williamson Furnace operated until the beginning of the depression of 1892 at which time it was blown out and not again operated until the turn of the century.

The Williamson Iron Co. was a fair weather plant. Due to lack of coal and ore, the operating cost was prohibitive save during times of high prices. Coke was secured from the Lewisburg and Coalburg mines and both red hematite from Red Mountain and brown hematite from Tuscaloosa County had to be purchased from various mining companies. At one time, however, the Sloss Company supplied the red hematite while its City Furnaces were inactive.

The Jones Valley Iron Co. leased the Williamson Furnace and operated it in 1900 and 1901. At that time a portion of the brown hematite ore was obtained from Jenifer in Talladega County. After about two years operation the plant was blown out again in 1903 and stayed idle until 1906 when it was again operated for a period of about a year until the panic of 1907 caused a shutdown. The Williamson Furnace Co. was organized and ran the plant on lease during 1910 and part of 1911, after which time the furnace was idle until dismantled in 1917-18.

The old Williamson Furnace is an illustration of the small, non-integrated, independent plant which could operate only in times of high prices and which today has passed from the picture.

Letterhead of Woodstock Iron & Steel Co., showing the charcoal furnaces as they appeared about 1880. Note totally enclosed furnace stacks.

WOODSTOCK FURNACES
Anniston, Calhoun County
No. 1—April 13, 1873
No. 2—August 23, 1879
No. A—October 10, 1889
No. B—June 6, 1892

IN 1854 the Noble family moved from Pennsylvania to Rome, Ga. and built there the first large foundry and machine shop in the Southeastern states. The first locomotive constructed south of the Mason-Dixon line was built at this shop in 1857. At the outbreak of the Civil War the Nobles began manufacturing heavy ordnance for the Confederate Government. Union forces however destroyed the plant at Rome in 1865. The Nobles had also built the Cornwall furnace in Cherokee County, Alabama to supply their foundry but that too had been demolished.

After the war and when internal conditions had somewhat improved, Samuel Noble determined to buy a site near the ruins of the old Oxford Furnace in Calhoun County to develop the adjacent brown hematite deposits. Gen. Daniel Tyler, then a man of about 70 years, became interested in the venture and with Tyler's financial backing the Woodstock Iron Co. was organized. This company, formed in 1872, was headed by Tyler with Noble as General Superintendent.

So acute was the lack of skilled labor at that time that James Noble, a brother of Samuel, had to go to Europe for the purpose of procuring workmen. Stone masons, brick masons and furnacemen were brought from England; charcoal burners from Sweden. A little community was formed which of necessity had to be as nearly self-supporting as possible. Houses for the workmen were first built, then a flour and grist mill, and finally a little iron shelled charcoal furnace which went into blast on April 13, 1873. This furnace was 43′ high and 12′ across the bosh. All of its machinery was made in Rome by the Nobles at their machine shop. The furnace was equipped with a cast iron pipe stove but an old letter-head states: *"Blast, Hot or Cold, can change to Cold Blast in a few minutes."*

The Woodstock plant was located not more than 300 yards north of the ruined Oxford furnace and within the present corporate limits of the City of Anniston. The Selma, Rome and Dalton Railroad terminated at Blue Mountain, just north of the plant. Within half a mile of the furnace was a deposit of brown hematite and the forests of the adjoining country furnished charcoal.

The Woodstock plant went into blast just as the panic of 1873 closed in on the iron industry and the price of pig iron fell abruptly from $40 a ton to less than half that figure. By borrowing money at 13% against iron on the yard the Woodstock Company, however, continued to operate. When the storm of depression passed, the new company was in a favorable condition to supply the increased demand. Most of its output went into car wheels at plants both North and South. It is said that the first Spiegleisen made in the United States was produced here in 1874-75. In 1880 the Directory of the American Iron & Steel Association lists the Woodstock products as "car wheel pig iron and Spiegeleisen."

A second and larger charcoal furnace was begun late in 1878. The No. 2 went into blast Aug. 23, 1879. It was 50′ high, 12′ in the bosh and 5½′ in the hearth. Like the smaller No. 1, this stack had a sand-stone hearth. As was the case with several other furnaces of Alabama, both these stacks were enclosed in a wooden building which was extended to include the cast house.

In 1880 the No. 1 furnace was enlarged to 54′ in height and 11½′ in the bosh and the combined capacity of the two furnaces was increased to 25,000 tons annually. At this time an average of 108 bu. of charcoal were required to produce a ton of iron. At that rate the furnaces were consuming 2,700,000 bu. of charcoal a year. As a consequence of this large consumption it became necessary to get wood from greater and greater distances and the cost of iron produced here rapidly increased.

Woodstock Coke Furnaces Nos. "A" and "B" in Anniston, about 1895.

It soon became obvious to all that the day of the charcoal furnace was doomed. Realizing this, Samuel Noble began in 1888 the building of a coke furnace on the other side of Anniston (about 3 miles) from the charcoal furnaces. In that same year he helped organize the Anniston Pipe Works Co. Noble was an ardent advocate of local consumption and preached that the salvation of the South lay in industrial independence. He died in 1888 but the many enterprises to which he set his hand lived on.

The new coke furnace, as Furnace "A", went into blast Oct. 10, 1889. Its stack was 75' x 16'. In order to have a constant source of fuel supply the Woodstock Co. bought an interest in the Cahaba Coal and Mining Co. and helped finance construction of 400 beehive ovens at the Blocton mines.

The fourth Anniston furnace, Furnace "B", went into blast June 12, 1892 and was an exact duplicate of Furnace "A". Less than a year later the depression of 1893 arrived and the furnaces were blown out. The Woodstock Iron Co. had expanded to such a great extent that it never fully recovered. In addition to furnaces, this company had built a railroad, numerous manufacturing plants and a large city. The old charcoal furnace No. 2 had been partially destroyed by fire in 1891 and in

1892 the No. 1 was blown out. The No. 2 was dismantled in 1894 and the No. 1 in 1898. Furnace "A" was rebuilt in 1900 and the "B" was rebuilt in 1896, the combined capacity of the plant being 150,000 tons annually.

On November 15, 1906 a new company, the Woodstock Iron & Steel Corp., acquired the property and put Furnace "A" into blast. Furnace "B" was not in operating condition at that time. This company also constucted a battery of beehive coke ovens at the plant. The furnace was operated intermittedly for two years, then shut down.

The Anniston Iron Corp. was organized with capital of $600,000 on March 24, 1910 by a group of Lynchburg, Va. pipe manufacturers to purchase the Woodstock property. Furnace "A" was remodeled by this corporation and put into blast. Both red ore from Jefferson County and brown ore (hematite) from East Alabama were shipped in as well as coke from the Birmingham district. High cost of raw material transportation made the Woodstock operation almost prohibitive except in a period of great pig iron demand and very high prices. In consequence the furnace was blown out during 1912.

In 1916 the Woodstock Operating Corp. was formed and leased the Woodstock Furnaces for a period of three years. In July of 1917 the Woodstock Operating Corp. purchased the entire property from the Woodstock Iron & Steel Corp. Furnace "B" was dismantled in 1918 after being idle for about 15 years. Furnace "A" was rebuilt in 1919 and enlarged to 78' x 17'. The furnace was blown in during 1919 and operated until late in 1920, thereafter remaining idle until dismantled in 1924-25.

Original Woodward Furnace No. 1. Picture taken in Fall of 1882.

WOODWARD FURNACES
Woodward, Jefferson County
No. 1—Aug. 17, 1883
No. 2—Jan. 26, 1887
No. 3—June 23, 1905

ONE day in February, 1867, while aboard an Ohio river steamboat, S. H. Woodward overheard two Union soldiers discussing the ore and coal deposits which they had seen during the Alabama campaign. Woodward was an iron-master of Wheeling, West Virginia and could appreciate the value of the information. Two years later, in January 1869, he made his first trip into the state of Alabama. After inspecting the brown ore deposits at Shelby and the red ore vein of Jefferson County, he purchased 550 acres of ore land on Red Mountain on January 30, 1869. Within two weeks he also purchased more than $30,000 worth of additional coal and ore lands. A little later that same year he bought a tract of about 2,000 acres of brown ore land in Tuscaloosa County near Woodstock. This property, acquired in 1869, became the nucleus of the Woodward Iron Co.

Hearing that the Eureka Company (Oxmoor Furnaces) were planning to substitute coke for charcoal in its furnaces, S. H. Woodward sent his son J. H. Woodward to Alabama where he spent the Winter of 1875 and the Spring of 1876 observing the Oxmoor operation. Apparently the test at Oxmoor was not conclusive because J. H. Woodward advised his father that it was not yet time to develop their property.

When the Alice Furnace at Birmingham went into blast in 1880, once again S. H. Woodward sent a son into Alabama, this time W. H. Woodward. This son's observations convinced the elder Woodward that coke iron could be successfully and profitably produced in Jefferson County.

Plans were made accordingly to begin development of the Alabama mineral property but while these were in progress S. H. Woodward died. His sons carried on and the Woodward Iron Company was organized in the Fall of 1881 with W. H. Woodward as President and J. H. Woodward as Secretary-Treasurer.

A site for the proposed blast furnace was chosen midway between the ore vein on the southeast and the coal field on the northwest of the property. This tract, about 12 miles southeast of Birmingham, was purchased from Fleming Jordan in the Spring of 1882. The Woodward brothers brought with them $400,000 in cash with which to build a blast furnace, 150 beehive ovens, open both ore and coal mines, and construct about eight miles of railroad. Before any of the foregoing could be commenced, it was first necessary to construct houses for the workmen, a store, and a brick kiln. All the brick used in the construction of the elevator tower, cast shed, company store and office were made on the furnace yard. In the early Spring of 1882, ground was broken for erection of the first Woodward furnace, which went into blast August 17, 1883. Height of this furnace was 75′ and the bosh was 17′ in diameter.

In 1886 J. H. Woodward succeeded his brother, W. H. Woodward as president of the Woodward Iron Company. During that same year a second blast furnace was begun. This stack, also 75′ x 17′, went into blast January 26, 1887. The two furnaces had a combined capacity of about 165 tons daily. Increased consumption of fuel by the two furnaces necessitated opening a second coal mine on the Pratt Seam (¾ mile north of No. 1 slope). The number of beehive coke ovens was likewise increased to 365. At this time ore cost 68c a ton delivered and coal 80c a ton. A very low cost on pig iron was possible at Woodward because of the proximity of raw materials and low cost assembly of materials over the company's railroad.

Woodward blast furnaces Nos. 1, 2 and 3, with employees' houses in foreground.

During the panic of 1893 which put more furnaces out of blast in Alabama than any condition before or since, and brought scrip into general use because of the money scarcity, the Woodward Company managed to continue operations.

A third furnace was begun by Woodward in 1903 and blown in on June 23, 1905. This stack was 85' high and 20' in the bosh. In 1906-7 the No. 2 furnace was enlarged to the same dimensions as the new No. 3, the combined capacity of the three furnaces being then rated at 250,000 tons annually. To supply the coke for the increased operation 772 beehive ovens were utilized.

A new slope, the Red Ore No. 2, was driven on the red hematite vein in 1905 to furnish the ore for the new furnace. In that same year the Docray brown ore mine near Woodstock, was developed but did not get into full production until 1908.

In 1911 the Woodward Iron Company installed its first battery of 60 by-product coke ovens and a year later built an additional 80 ovens.

In 1912 the company acquired the Birmingham Coal and Iron Company. Purchase of that company added the two Vanderbilt Furnaces, two coal mines, 310 beehive coke ovens, and the Songo red ore mine to Woodward's operations. However, the most important feature of the purchase was acquisition of immense coal reserves.

With the outbreak of the World War all Woodward furnaces were blown to capacity tonnage. To meet the greatly increased war-time demand, the Woodward Iron Company constructed a battery of 90 new by-product coke ovens and abandoned all its beehive ovens. A new coal mine slope, Dolomite No. 3 was also opened on the Pratt seam in 1918 to supply the enlarged furnace demands.

Since the World War the Woodward Company has remodeled and rebuilt its furnaces a number of times. In 1939 this company installed the country's first modern de-humidifying system for controlling the moisture content of the air blown into the furnace, an installation which has proved signally successful.

Since the first small, hand-filled furnace went into blast in August 1883, the Woodward Iron Company has produced more than 12,500,000 tons of pig iron. The company has ore and coal reserves adequate to operate its three blast furnaces at peak capacity for more than a century. The Woodward Iron Company ranks today as the largest independent and completely integrated manufacturer of merchant pig iron in the United States.

CHRONOLOGICAL TABLE

Name of Furnace	Where Located	Date First Blown In
*Cedar Creek Furnace	Franklin County	1815
*Cane Creek Furnace	Calhoun County	1840
*Little Cahaba Furnace No. 1	Bibb County	about 1848
†Shelby Furnace No. 1	Shelby County	Spring 1849
*Round Mountain Furnace	Cherokee County	April 1852
*Hale & Murdock Furnace	Lamar County	1859
*Tannehill Furnace No. 1	Tuscaloosa County	1859-1861
*Bibb Furnace No. 1	Bibb County	1861
*Cornwall Furnace	Cherokee County	1862-1863
†Shelby Furnace No. 2	Shelby County	March 1863
†Bibb Furnace No. 2	Bibb County	1863
*Oxford Furnace	Calhoun County	April, 1863
*Little Cahaba Furnace No. 2	Bibb County	about 1863
†Oxmoor Furnace No. 1	Jefferson County	Nov. 1863
†Jenifer Furnace	Talladega County	1863
*Tannehill Furnaces Nos. 2 & 3	Tuscaloosa County	1863
*Knight Furnace	Talladega County	1863-1864
†Irondale Furnace	Jefferson County	1863-1864
*Woodstock Furnace No. 1	Calhoun County	April 13, 1873
†Stonewall Furnace	Cherokee County	1873
†Oxmoor Furnace No. 2	Jefferson County	Fall of 1873
*Tecumseh Furnace	Cherokee County	Feb. 19, 1874
*Rock Run Furnace	Cherokee County	June 1, 1874
*Woodstock Furnace No. 2	Calhoun County	Aug. 23, 1879
Edwards Furnace	Bibb County	June 10, 1880
Alice Furnace No. 1	Jefferson County	Nov. 23, 1880
Sloss City Furnace No. 1	Jefferson County	April 12, 1882
Mary Pratt Furnace	Jefferson County	April, 1883
*Gadsden Furnace	Etowah County	May 30, 1883
Alice Furnace No. 2	Jefferson County	July 24, 1883
Woodward Furnace No. 1	Jefferson County	Aug. 17, 1883
Sloss City Furnace No. 2	Jefferson County	Oct. 1883
*Ironaton Furnace No. 1	Talladega County	April 16, 1885
Williamson Furnace	Jefferson County	Oct. 1886
Woodward Furnace No. 2	Jefferson County	Jan. 26, 1887
Hattie Ensley Furnace	Colbert County	Dec. 31, 1887
Ensley Furnace No. 4	Jefferson County	April 9, 1888
Thomas Furnace No. 1	Jefferson County	May 15, 1888
Ensley Furnace No. 3	Jefferson County	June 5, 1888
Bessemer Furnace No. 1	Jefferson County	June, 1888
Cole Furnace No. 1	Colbert County	Sept. 1888
Etowah Furnace No. 1	Etowah County	Oct. 14, 1888
Sloss Furnace No. 3 (North Birmingham No. 1)	Jefferson County	Oct. 1888

Name of Furnace	Where Located	Date First Blown In
Ensley Furnace No. 2	Jefferson County	Dec. 1, 1888
Sloss Furnace No. 4 (North Birmingham No. 2)	Jefferson County	Feb. 1889
Ensley Furnace No. 1	Jefferson Count	April 29, 1889
Lady Ensley Furnace	Colbert County	April 25, 1889
Bessemer Furnace No. 2	Jefferson County	April 1889
Trussville Furnace	Jefferson County	April 1889
†Attalla Furnace	Etowah County	June 10, 1889
Talladega Furnace	Talladega County	Oct. 5, 1889
Woodstock Furnace No. A	Calhoun County	Oct. 10, 1889
Cole Furnace No. 2	Colbert County	Oct. 1889
North Alabama Furnace	Lauderdale County	Oct. 1889
Thomas Furnace No. 2	Jefferson County	Feb. 22, 1890
†Decatur Furnace	Morgan County	Feb. 23, 1890
Vanderbilt Furnace No. 1	Jefferson County	Aug. 23, 1890
Fort Payne Furnace	DeKalb County	Sept. 3, 1890
Robertstown No. 1 Furnace	Jefferson County	1890
Robertstown No. 2 Furnace	Jefferson County	1890
Little Bell Furnace	Jefferson County	1890
Philadelphia Furnace	Lauderdale County	Spring of 1891
†Ironaton No. 2 Furnace	Talladega County	July 1891
Woodstock Furnace No. B	Calhoun County	June 6, 1892
Cole Furnace No. 3	Colbert County	April 1895
Ensley Furnace No. 5	Jefferson County	Nov. 15, 1900
Thomas Furnace No. 3	Jefferson County	June 13, 1902
Holt Furnace	Tuscaloosa County	Aug. 1, 1903
Etowah Furnace No. 2	Etowah County	Aug. 22, 1903
Alabama City Furnace	Etowah County	Jan. 17, 1904
Battelle Furnace	DeKalb County	Sept. 10, 1904
Ensley Furnace No. 6	Jefferson County	April 28, 1905
Woodward Furnace No. 3	Jefferson County	June 23, 1905
Vanderbilt Furnace No. 2	Jefferson County	May 8, 1908
Fairfield Furnace No. 5	Jefferson County	June 25, 1928
Fairfield Furnace No. 6	Jefferson County	Sept. 27, 1928

Following four furnaces commenced but not operated:

*Montgomery Furnace	Montgomery County	Begun 1887
*Piedmont Furnace	Calhoun County	Abandoned 1891
Bay State Furnace	DeKalb County	Abandoned 1891
*Janney Furnace	Calhoun County	Destroyed 1864

*Charcoal Furnace.

†Charcoal and Coke Furnace.

PRODUCTION OF PIG IRON IN ALABAMA

Year	Gross Tons	Year	Gross Tons
1840	30	1905	1,604,062
1850	522	1906	1,674,848
1872	11,171	1907	1,686,694
1873	19,895	1908	1,397,014
1874	29,342	1909	1,763,617
1875	22,418	1910	1,939,147
1876	22,080	1911	1,617,150
1877	36,823	1912	1,987,753
1878	37,037	1913	1,924,762
1879	44,500	1914	1,661,420
1880	68,995	1915	2,065,483
1881	97,590	1916	2,753,824
1882	100,683	1917	2,936,594
1883	153,987	1918	2,546,289
1884	169,342	1919	2,111,381
1885	203,069	1920	2,376,864
1886	253,445	1921	1,201,138
1887	261,394	1922	2,215,832
1888	401,330	1923	2,780,488
1889	706,629	1924	2,748,702
1890	816,911	1925	2,815,728
1891	795,672	1926	2,933,796
1892	915,296	1927	2,762,810
1893	726,888	1928	2,517,485
1894	592,392	1929	2,704,733
1895	854,667	1930	2,382,221
1896	922,170	1931	1,640,851
1897	947,831	1932	652,898
1898	1,033,676	1933	900,170
1899	1,103,905	1934	1,171,650
1900	1,184,337	1935	1,297,960
1901	1,225,212	1936	1,998,212
1902	1,472,211	1937	2,580,674
1903	1,561,408	1938	2,023,269
1904	1,453,513	1939	2,614,231

For this tabulation of pig iron production in Alabama we are indebted to:

Alabama Geological Survey—1872-1910.
Department of the Interior—1910-1939.
Department of Commerce—1840-1850.
Birmingham Chamber of Commerce—1900-1939.

INDEX

INDEX—(Continued)

INDEX—(Continued)

INDEX—(Continued)

INDEX—(Continued)